Coordinating science
across the primary school

THE SUBJECT LEADER'S HANDBOOKS

Series Editor: Mike Harrison, Centre for Primary Education,
School of Education, The University of Manchester,
Oxford Road, Manchester, M13 9DP

Coordinating mathematics across the primary school
Tony Brown

Coordinating English at Key Stage 1
Mick Waters and Tony Martin

Coordinating English at Key Stage 2
Mick Waters and Tony Martin

Coordinating science across the primary school
Lynn D. Newton and Douglas P. Newton

Coordinating information technology across the primary school
Mike Harrison

Coordinating art across the primary school
Judith Piotrowski, Robert Clements and Ivy Roberts

Coordinating design and technology across the primary school
Alan Cross

Coordinating geography across the primary school
John Halocha

Coordinating history across the primary school
Julie Davies and Jason Redmond

Coordinating music across the primary school
Sarah Hennessy

Coordinating religious education across the primary school
Derek Bastide

Coordinating physical education across the primary school
Carole Raymond

Management skills for SEN coordinators
Sylvia Phillips, Jennifer Goodwin and Rosita Heron

Building a whole school assessment policy
Mike Wintle and Mike Harrison

The curriculum coordinator and the OFSTED inspection
Phil Gadsby and Mike Harrison

Coordinating the curriculum in the smaller primary school
Mick Waters

Coordinating science across the primary school

Lynn D. Newton and Douglas P. Newton

FALMER PRESS
Taylor & Francis Group

UK	The Falmer Press, 1 Gunpowder Square, London, EC4A 3DE
USA	The Falmer Press, Taylor & Francis Inc., 1900 Frost Road, Suite 101, Bristol, PA 19007

First published in 1998

A catalogue record for this book is available from the British Library

ISBN 0 7507 0688 0 paper

Library of Congress Cataloging-in-Publication Data are available on request

Jacket design by Carla Turchini

Typeset in 10/14pt Melior and printed by Graphicraft Typesetters Ltd., Hong Kong

Every effort has been made to contact copyright holders for their permission to reprint material in this book. The publishers would be grateful to hear from any copyright holder who is not here acknowledged and will undertake to rectify any errors or omissions in future editions of this book.

Contents

Part one
The role of the science coordinator

Part two
What science coordinators need to know

Part three
Whole school policies and schemes of work

Part four
Monitoring for quality

Part five
Resources for learning

List of figures

This book has been prepared for primary teachers charged with the responsibility of acting as science coordinators within their schools. It forms part of a series of new publications that set out to advise such teachers on the complex issues of improving teaching and learning through managing each element of the primary school curriculum.

Why is there a need for such a series? Most authorities recognise, after all, that the quality of primary children's work and learning depends upon the skills of their class teacher, not in the structure of management systems, policy documents or the titles and job descriptions of staff. Many today recognise that school improvement equates directly to the improvement of teaching so surely all tasks, other than imparting subject knowledge, are merely a distraction for the committed primary teacher.

Nothing should take teachers away from their most important role, that is, serving the best interests of the class of children in their care and this book and the others in the series does not wish to diminish that mission. However, the increasing complexity of the primary curriculum and society's expanding expectations, makes it very difficult for the class teacher to keep up to date with every development. Within traditional subject areas there has been an explosion of knowledge and new fields introduced such as science, technology, design, problem solving and health education, not to mention the uses of computers. These are now considered entitlements for primary children. Furthermore, we now expect all children to succeed at these studies, not just the fortunate few. All this has overwhelmed a class teacher system largely unchanged since the inception of primary schools.

Primary class teachers cannot possibly be an expert in every aspect of the curriculum they are required to teach. To whom can they turn for help? It is unrealisitic to assume that such support will be available from the headteacher whose responsibilities have grown ever wider since the 1988 Educational Reform Act. Constraints, including additional staff costs, and the loss of benefits from the strength and security of the class teacher system, militate against wholesale adoption of specialist or semi-specialist teaching. Help therefore has to come from exploiting the talents of teachers themselves, in a process of mutual support. Hence primary schools have chosen many and varied systems of consultancy or subject coordination which best suit the needs of their children and the current expertise of the staff.

In fact, curriculum leadership functions in primary schools have increasingly been shared with class teachers through the policy of curriculum coordination for the past twenty years, especially to improve the consistency of work in language and mathematics. Since then each school has developed their own system and the series recognises that the system each reader is part of will be a compromise between the ideal and the possible. Campbell and Neill (1944) show that by 1991 nearly nine out of every ten primary class teachers had such responsibility and the average number of subjects each was between 1.5 and 2.2 (depending on the size of school).

These are the people for whom this series sets out to help to do this part of their work. The books each deal with specific issues whilst at the same time providing an overview of general themes in the management of the subject curriculum. The term *subject leader* is used in an inclusive sense and combines the two major roles that such teachers play when they have responsibility for subjects and aspects of the primary curriculum.

The books each deal with:
- coordination — a role which emphasises harmonising, bringing together, making links, establishing routines and common practice; and
- subject leadership — a role which emphasises providing information, offering expertise and direction, guiding the development of the subject, and raising standards.

The purpose of the series is to give practical guidance and support to teachers; in particular what to do and how to do it. They each offer help on the production, development and review of policies and schemes of work; the organisation of resources; and developing strategies for improving the management of the subject curriculum.

Each book in the series contains material that subject managers will welcome and find useful in developing their subject expertise and in tackling problems of enthusing and motivating staff.

Each book has five parts.
1 The review and development of the different roles coordinators are asked to play.
2 Updating subject knowledge and subject pedagogical knowledge.
3 Developing and maintaining policies and schemes of work.
4 Monitoring work within the school to enhance the continuity of teaching and progression in pupil's learning.
5 Resources and contacts.

Although written primarily for teachers who are science coordinators, Lynn and Douglas Newton's book offers practical guidance and many insights into science teaching for anyone in the school who has a responsibility for the science curriculum, including teachers with an overall role in coordinating the whole or key stage curriculum and the deputy head and headteacher.

In making the book easily readable they have drawn upon their considerable experience as teacher educators and researchers and their extensive experience in writing on science issues. As an external examiner at their institution I witnessed the enthusiasm with which they infected their ITT students for teaching science to young children. They were also much in demand as service providers and their advice in this book will be invaluable to those attempting to develop a whole-school view of progress in science, particularly those who are new to the job or have recently changed schools. This book lives up to my expectations and will help readers develop both the subject expertise they will need and the managerial perspective necessary to enthuse others. Enjoy it.

Mike Harrison, Series Editor
January 1998

Coordinating primary school science

Over a decade ago, the then Chairman of the Association for Science Education wrote in the editorial introduction to the first issue of the *Primary Science Review*:

❛ *Bringing about change in the educational world is rarely easy. Well established and familiar practices die hard; our system is complex and it is not often that we are able to bring the necessary resources to bear. These are all very good reasons for standing still or at best moving forward very slowly. There are, however, some imperatives for change which, despite the inertia of the system, refuse to give up.* (Nellist, 1986, p. 2)

John Nellist was, of course, referring to the development of science teaching in primary schools. Accompanying this development has been the evolution of teachers with responsibility for bringing about such change — the science coordinators.

Even before the introduction of the National Curriculum for Science, interest in and justification for its inclusion in the primary school curriculum was gathering momentum. Various initiatives, like the government's 40-day courses for science coordinators and the Educational Support Grant programme, were paving the way. This momentum has been given direction by the introduction of the National Curriculum and resulted in OFSTED inspectors concluding that:

> ❝ *In primary schools science and technology have been the most significant areas of curricular growth during the last decade. Science now has an established place in the primary school curriculum.* (OFSTED, 1994a, p. 17)

However, evidence from more recent inspection reports indicates that there is no cause for complacency in the primary science world. Indeed, the comments Nellist made over a decade ago about science could equally well describe the task facing the science coordinator today. The role is one of bringing about change with meagre resources and, at the same time, supporting colleagues sensitively, both those who want to stand still and those who are keen to move on. At the same time, the science coordinator in most schools will be a class teacher with all that that role involves and with probably little or no non-teaching time for self-development or time to help colleagues.

The science coordinator's task

If you already are, or hope soon to be, a science coordinator then this book is written with you in mind. It aims to give you a clearer understanding of what you can expect in your role as a science coordinator and how you can develop this role at both the personal and school levels. In the OFSTED *Handbook for the Inspection of Schools* (1993), a coordinator is defined as:

> ❝ *. . . a teacher responsible for leading and co-ordinating the teaching and learning within a subject, curricular area or key stage . . .* (p. 29)

So, what qualities will you need to be successful in this role? The first point to make is that as a coordinator you do not have to be superhuman — or at least no more so than any other effective class teacher. No-one else expects you to be perfect so do not expect it of yourself. You do need to know what your role involves and what is expected of you, so ask questions and find out more about the job description. Also, determine what your working relationship with the headteacher and with other coordinators will be. Voice your feeling about anything that you have any doubts about or feel unsure of. If you accept the role of coordinator, take it on as a challenge to be enjoyed, adding to your own development.

You do need to be well organised and in command of both the skills, knowledge and understanding which underpin primary school science (subject knowledge) and how to teach these effectively (implementation knowledge). Science presents its own unique problems in that it is not just one subject (as with history or English), it is multi-dimensional, incorporating several areas of science. Therefore, even if you have some knowledge of one area (Biology, Chemistry, Physics, Geology, or Astronomy), you are unlikely to be a specialist in all. The National Curriculum Order for Science incorporates all, so you will need a broad and balanced science knowledge base.

Good interpersonal skills are also essential, as you will need to relate to people in appropriate ways. You must also be an effective communicator with individuals, groups and larger audiences. Communication involves listening as well as talking and writing, and so you need to be a good listener. The personal touch works best with most people and your colleagues are likely to be no exception. They are more likely to respond to things if addressed personally rather than in writing and most like to have their views considered and to be involved in decisions. Teachers, children, governors and parents respond better if something catches their interest so plan carefully how you communicate ideas and information.

Harrison (1996) recommends that coordinators have an ability to:
- act consistently;
- maintain hope, belief and optimism;
- want success, though not necessarily approval;
- take risks;
- use conflict constructively;
- use a soft voice and keep interactions low key;
- develop self-awareness;
- tolerate ambiguity and complexity;
- avoid seeing things as black and white.

These qualities and skills are likely to be used to bring about changes of various kinds. There are three major areas most science coordinators have to think about. First, some staff will lack confidence in their own abilities to teach science. It may be that their science backgrounds are limited and so they will need support from you in various ways. This can range from help with ideas and planning through to resource management and demonstrations to show what can be done.

Second, science is an active process, involving first-hand experience and practical investigation which may result in movement and some noise. This may be contrary to some teachers' normal practices and accommodating such different ways of working may need time and support. It may also generate problems of management and organisation which will have to be addressed.

Third, with the rapid changes that are occurring in initial teacher education it is quite likely that newly qualified teachers are entering the profession with significantly more science training than many of their colleagues in schools. As such, they are less likely to need your help and support than some of your older colleagues who have been teaching for a number of years. It is also possible that you may be one of these younger teachers, who has achieved the role of coordinator for science fairly quickly. As such, you may well find yourself in the position of having to provide support and advice to your older, more experienced colleagues. This is going to require a great deal of patience, tact and diplomacy and also an acceptance on your part that with some colleagues progress will be slow.

Even if you inherit a sound science policy, effectively implemented by a team of committed colleagues, monitoring, fine tuning and change will still be necessary. Teachers leave and new teachers arrive, inspection cycles come around, new resources become available, government documents identify curriculum changes to be made, assessment results show inconsistencies across the school or some in-service training stimulates a desire to change.

Suggestion

If you are about to apply for a post of responsibility as a science coordinator, or have recently been appointed to such a post, you could read Chapter 1 to gain a feel for what is involved in the role. This will give you some starting points for discussion.

Harrison (1996) suggests that a climate for change can be created by:
- emphasising aspects of good practice;
- displaying articles and reviews;
- inviting speakers into school;
- running workshops;
- looking at and trying out new materials as a staff;
- reporting on meetings and courses attended.

The various HMI reports (for example, DES, 1978; DES, 1984; DES, 1989; HMI, 1991) point to differences in the quality of science experiences offered in schools, differences not only between schools but also between classrooms in the same school. As the science coordinator, you must ensure that a consistently high quality is maintained throughout the school. This means that you will have responsibilities which go across the school, even though you yourself may have been trained to teach Infants (Key Stage 1) or Juniors (Key Stage 2). As the coordinator, you must make yourself aware of the work and levels of experiences appropriate for other ages so that you can promote progression and continuity as well as support colleagues.

This book is intended to help you to fulfil this complex role. Chapter 1 provides you with a general overview of the role of the science coordinator. The remaining chapters consider in more detail the different dimensions of your role, what might be expected of you and how you can meet these expectations.

Throughout, there are a number of suggestion boxes. These are intended to focus your attention on things you might think about or information you might collect and also provide you with ideas for discussions with colleagues and suggestions for staff development sessions.

Part one | The role of the science coordinator

Chapter 1

The role of the science coordinator

Introduction

Prior to the introduction of the National Curriculum, science teaching in primary schools was variable in quantity and quality. Its inclusion in any significant way as part of the curriculum of primary schools is relatively recent, as is the notion of a teacher with a responsibility for coordinating science throughout the school. The first HMI report on Science in the National Curriculum indicated that although science was slowly becoming established in primary schools, there was still some way to go.

The main HMI findings were:

[a] work at key stage one tended to be in topic areas familiar to infant teachers and ignored the physical and earth sciences;

[b] science skill development was given a high priority but work was inadequately and insufficiently linked to subject knowledge;

[c] time spent on science was often inadequate;

[d] although schemes of work reflected National Curriculum requirements and teachers' planning had improved, they were unsure about important issues like assessment;

[e] almost half the schools visited had inadequate resources for science; and,

[g] the quality of the work in science was adversely affected by the lack of suitably qualified teachers in up to 20% of schools.

(from DES, 1991, para. 45, p. 27)

Suggestion

- Before you read the rest of this chapter, jot down the things that you think will be expected of you in your role as science coordinator.
- Sort your list into an order of importance according to what you feel will be your priorities.
- Beside each item or cluster on your prioritised list, identify what you feel you would need to achieve this (e.g. time, money, outside help, and so on).
- Put the list to one side to review later when you have finished reading the chapter.

HMI concluded that a well-trained and knowledgeable science coordinator was essential for National Curriculum success. A similar conclusion had been reached by their colleagues over a decade earlier from the HMI survey of primary education:

> ❝ *... where a teacher with a special responsibility was able to exercise it through the planning and supervision of a programme of work, this was effective in raising the standards of work and the levels of expectation of what children were capable of doing.* (DES, 1978, para. 4.6)

Thus, an informed and effective science coordinator is crucial if primary schools are to lay sound foundations on which children's science education is built.

So what is a science coordinator and what might be expected of you if you become one? This chapter provides a broad overview of the role of the science coordinator in a primary school. It could serve as a straightforward introduction for anyone thinking about or being interviewed for a post of responsibility for science. Subsequent chapters will provide more detailed information about various aspects of this role. Once you have been given the responsibility, they will provide support in translating ideas into practice.

Being a science coordinator

When you hold a post of responsibility for science, you may well find yourself being given one of several titles:

- *the science specialist teacher*: someone with some subject expertise in an aspect of science, probably with academic qualifications, and who may be asked to teach science to other classes;
- *the science curriculum leader*: someone who probably has a subject specialism in science and who can provide advice on the subject itself, guidance on how to teach it throughout the school, and who perhaps teaches science to some other classes as well;
- *the science curriculum manager*: someone who has administrative skills and perhaps some subject expertise, although not necessarily any academic qualifications in

science, and who can take responsibility for the structure, form and direction of science throughout the school;

■ *the science curriculum coordinator*: someone who is likely to have science expertise, and can coordinate the teaching and learning of science throughout the school and provide support and guidance to colleagues as needed.

In reality, as the school's science coordinator, you are likely to be all of these and probably much more and it is with this broader coordinator's role, rather than the science specialist teacher role, that this book is concerned.

If you are the science coordinator, it is important to remember that you may have colleagues who are also science specialists. You should use this to your advantage, since they are another source of support to both yourself and to the school, especially if their science specialism complements rather than mirrors your own. In addition, there will be other colleagues on the staff who are curriculum leaders, managers and specialists, and who are quite likely to have had to deal with many of the issues of leadership, management and coordination which you now face. Once again, see them as people to talk to who may be able to advise you about generic matters rather than subject specific ones. This will help you as you develop your role.

The dimensions of the science coordinator's role

Haigh (1996) described effective primary subject coordinators as the rising stars of the staffroom, yet he noted that,

❝ *The primary co-ordinator's position seems ill defined when compared with that of a secondary head of department — there is rarely a physical empire of rooms and resources nor the opportunity to recruit and lead a team of fellow-specialists. The title 'co-ordinator' seems to have been deliberately chosen for its slightly vague, non-authoritarian associations.* (p. 6)

In 1992, Bell reported that although the number of primary schools with a teacher responsible for developing and coordinating science throughout the school had increased significantly in the previous decade, they were not having the impact they should have on the quality of science in schools. Drawing on discussions he had with head teachers, class teachers and science coordinators, Bell concluded that this was partly due to a limited view of the role of the coordinator. He could find few descriptions of the role of such teachers. However, he reported the work of Morrison (1986), who produced a synthesis of all the various descriptions then available and ranked the characteristics of the role in order of perceived importance.

Aspects of the coordinator's role (Morrison, 1986):
- communicate with the headteacher;
- exercise curriculum leadership;
- communicate with staff;
- organise resources;
- establish continuity throughout the school;
- organise in-service training;
- liaise between head and staff;
- establish record systems;
- motivate staff; and,
- promote curriculum development.

While Bell generally agreed with Morrison's list of the characteristics of the role, he pointed out that:

 ... there are some specific demands made on individual co-ordinators which are closely related to the nature of their particular curriculum area. Science perhaps makes greater demands than other areas. (Bell, 1992, p. 96)

Demands on the science coordinator can arise from:
- the essential practical nature of science education which requires resources and equipment;
- the safety considerations which practical activity in science necessitates;
- the need for the development by teachers of personal scientific knowledge and understanding;
- the fact that many teachers lack confidence and training in science work.

A useful starting point when thinking about your role is *Science 5–16: A statement of policy* (DES, 1985), in which the science coordinator's role is described in the following terms:

❛ *They can act as science consultants or experts in the primary school, stimulate science teaching throughout the school and provide help and support for their colleagues. This support may take the form of assistance with the preparation of programmes of work, individual lessons or materials, and it may involve taking on part of the teaching of some classes, for example with older pupils. Encouragement and support from the headteacher and from the LEA are also essential.*

(para. 21)

According to the discussion document, *Primary Matters* (OFSTED, 1994a), the official job description for a science coordinator would involve:

- developing a clear view of the nature of science and how it contributes to the wider curriculum;
- providing advice and documentation to help colleagues teach science and interrelate its constituent elements; and,
- playing a major part in organising the teaching of science and the resources available for science, so that the statutory requirements of the National Curriculum for Science are covered.

There are two central aspects to your role as a science coordinator to be considered. The first can be described as the static aspect of your role: supporting the current teaching of science in your school. The other is more dynamic: the pro-active development of high quality, effective science education throughout the school. Figure 1.1 summarises these two aspects of the role which, in practice, interact.

The remainder of this chapter will outline what each of these involves.

Support: maintaining science teaching and keeping it going

The aim of a science coordinator in the support role is to maintain a school's day-to-day science teaching. This

FIG 1.1
The role of the science
coordinator

SUPPORT: Maintaining Science	DEVELOPMENT: Promoting Science
Advising Colleagues: about science (*know what*) about teaching science (*know how*) **Managing Resources:** storage stock taking and ordering maintenance and repair safety audits **Liaising with Others:** your headteacher staff in your school staff in other schools advisory teachers LEA inspectors and HMI others, e.g. parents	**Keeping Yourself Informed:** awareness of new publications attending courses professional development **Disseminating Information to Others:** to staff to governors to parents staff development matters **Preparing and Reviewing Working Documents:** policy statement for science action plans scheme of work assessment and record keeping evaluation of learning

requires a drop of oil to keep the machine running, a road map, provisions for the journey, the removal of obstacles en route, monitoring progress, encouraging, and, occasionally, politely pushing. Consequently, you will have three things to think about:

■ advising and supporting colleagues;

■ managing resources;

■ liaising with others.

Advising and supporting colleagues

As the science coordinator, you will often have to respond to requests for science information (subject knowledge) and ideas for how to teach a topic (pedagogic knowledge). For example, questions range from, '*Yes, but . . . what exactly is energy?*' to '*How do I teach my class about the flow of electric current?*' This is not, however, the same as saying that you must be the fount of all science knowledge and understanding. Rather, what is needed is to know where to find the answers to such questions. In the first instance this may be from books so it is useful to have a small reference collection for basic information in a readily digestible form. However, guard against those old secondary school science textbooks which may serve as inappropriate models for primary practice.

Other questions likely to be asked of you relate to science education more broadly, such as, *'One of my topics this term is "Festivals". What can I do with my 6-year-olds in science that fits in with the National Curriculum?'* Alternatively, the whole school programme might say 'Chemical Changes' and the teacher says, *'There's a good television series on festivals this term which I would like to use. How can I bring the two together?'* The difficulty is apparent here. As the coordinator, you must be familiar with ideas and activities suitable for the full primary age range and ensure progression and continuity throughout the school, even though your personal experience may be limited to teaching one Key Stage. Textual resources can be supportive but so can other colleagues. It saves time and effort if successful ideas, areas of particular interest and expertise and plans for topics which have worked particularly well in the past are recorded in some way. A colleague who professes to know nothing about science may turn out to be a very keen angler who does some excellent science every year on life in rivers and ponds.

When such questions cannot be answered from such obvious sources, then it may be necessary for you to consult someone in the local authority advisory service. Chapter 3 looks in more detail at how the science coordinator works with other colleagues in different ways and for different purposes.

Managing resources

In science, resources will include materials and equipment for investigative work, information technology hardware and software, textual resources of various kinds and perhaps plants and animals. Their management could become a perennial problem for the coordinator unless a routine is established with which all staff are familiar. Equipment and materials may also have to be checked by you as part of a regular safety audit.

How resources are stored will be largely determined by their quantity, cost and security needs. For resources in sufficient quantity each teacher may have a stock in the classroom. For resources which are in short supply or which are more expensive, they will have to be shared and therefore a central store or cupboard will serve the purpose better. As far as school finances are concerned, the latter is a cheaper alternative. It may also be a more secure way of storing more expensive resources and be easier to monitor and control.

Whichever way the resources are stored, you will need to know what there is, where it is, and what condition it is in. Some regular check has to be made and a record kept of deficiencies, missing or damaged equipment and shortages. This can be easy in the case of a basic equipment box, which each teacher maintains in the classroom. A card fixed to the box can list the contents and each teacher can be responsible for checking it regularly. If resources are stored centrally, then a checking-out and checking-in system is needed.

While each teacher should check that all equipment, materials and practices are safe for their children to use and rectify or report problems or faults, stock-taking will give you the opportunity to monitor the provision of consumables like batteries or salt. Safety should be a paramount concern. The Association for Science Education (ASE, 1990) produce an excellent handbook on safety in primary school science, entitled *Be Safe*! Chapter 14 looks in more detail at ideas for organising and managing resources and carrying out safety audits.

Liaising with others

Usually, a school needs a link person to deal with outside bodies and individuals for matters relating to science. This is a useful responsibility for the coordinator since it can provide avenues for information, help, resources and, ultimately, should improve the quality of the science education in the school.

In some local education authorities, there are advisory teachers who are well-placed to help and inform. They may be able to support planning and give demonstration lessons, as well as offering guidance for new and returning teachers. In some LEAs, primary advisers have taken on curriculum consultancy roles, particularly in connection with preparation for inspection. They will often lead school-based in-service work to reinforce and develop good practice.

As the coordinator, you may need to liaise with colleagues in other schools, particularly in connection with the transfer of pupils from one to another. This may mean that programmes of work, the assessment evidence and the record keeping system for one school phase (for example, a first school, an infant school or a primary school) may need to articulate comfortably with those of the next phase (for example, a middle school or a junior school or a secondary school).

Evaluation of the educational experiences offered in a school may be by a team of LEA (local education authority) inspectors or by OFSTED. The information provided by subject coordinators resulting from your own internal evaluation procedures is important if they are to understand the unique situation of a school and provide a fair and worthwhile appraisal. Copies of the school's science policy, the whole school scheme of work, the assessment, recording and reporting system and how it applies to science, and the staff development programme should all be available. Portfolios containing samples of worksheets and children's work also provide a flavour of the quality of the science experiences throughout the school. The outcome of an appraisal should be sensitively used by you as the science coordinator to improve the school's science provision. Chapter 4 considers issues of school effectiveness and inspection.

Development: promoting science and moving them on

The aim of the coordinator as a curriculum developer is to identify and promote appropriate change in science education. This requires a keen eye for new routes, new destinations, and new modes of transport. Again, you will have three things to think about:

■ keeping yourself up to date and informed;

■ disseminating information to others; and,

■ preparing and reviewing working documents.

Keeping informed

Keeping informed is an active process of reading, listening and thinking about science and science education. As coordinator, you should receive, skim or read materials describing developments. Colleagues should be aware of your interests so that they might pass on information which comes to their attention by other means. If possible, you should arrange to receive a science teaching journal, such as *QMS* (*Questions of Maths and Science*) or *Primary Science Review*, the journal of the Association for Science Education (ASE) which has been published since 1986 and is now published five times a year.

Courses may also be vehicles for transmitting information on developments in science education. As well as those organised by local education authorities, check the mail from local universities and colleges to see what courses are on offer there, whether day-time or evening, and discuss with your headteacher who on the staff might benefit from attending, including yourself. Associations like the ASE also hold half-day and longer regional conferences two or three times a year to inform and update teachers generally and science coordinators in particular.

The school should be on the mailing list for free sources of information, such as those produced by industrial bodies like Shell and BP. For example, British Nuclear Fuels Limited (BNFL) in association with the Royal Microscopical Society, publishes a magazine of news, ideas and resources for primary school science and technology, called *The Young Detectives Magazine*.

Together, such sources contribute to your own professional development as science coordinator, and will help to make your support of colleagues more worthwhile, up to date and relevant. They can also make your role more interesting. Chapter 15 provides more details of such sources of support and information.

Disseminating information

The science coordinator must also keep colleagues informed about trends, changes and new ideas. This does not mean that teachers need to be burdened with details. Giving them a digest of what was said in a report or at a meeting prepares them for inevitable changes ahead and may take the feeling of threat out of change. You can do this informally over coffee in the staffroom, or in a more formal way by a brief presentation during a staff meeting. If space is available, you could also set up a science bulletin board on which information about courses, new publications, ideas, and so on, can be posted.

Such opportunities allow ideas to be tested and will give you the chance to see reactions. For something more significant, a special staff meeting or some training time might be used for this purpose. School-based staff development days allow time for new ideas to be studied in more depth, alternative practices to be agreed and new arrangements to be made. Such days may be used to examine new materials or new approaches to topics. They can also be used to consolidate and extend your colleagues' skills and knowledge base in science with sessions with a focus of, *'What is . . . and how can I teach it?'* The teachers themselves could each identify two or three aspects of science which they find difficult and the most frequently occurring ones can be addressed by you in this way.

Perceived relevance is an essential ingredient of success at such events. If the staff can see how they might use what they are doing, then they are more likely to cooperate and use what they learn. The advantage you have as the science coordinator is that you know the people and the situation in the school and so the activities can be designed to suit real and immediate needs and interests.

When parents value a subject they are more likely to support it and encourage their children to work well in it. Parents' perceptions, like teachers', will be coloured by their own experiences of science, particularly by their school memories, by the media and by the messages their children carry home. You can inform parents about the science education of their children in a number of ways: through a school newsletter; displays in school and public places like the library or sports centre; open afternoons; and, parents' evenings. The message should be clear, concise and jargon-free. It should point to both the short-term and long-term relevance of science education for their children. If possible, put examples of children's work on display as these catch attention and make the message more memorable. Finally, some coordinators run practical sessions for parents to let them try out some of the things their children do — first-hand experience for parents of what primary school science is all about.

Preparing and reviewing working documents

The coordinator usually has responsibility for developing the policy statement for science, although it may be part of the wider school policy for the whole curriculum. It needs to be a succinct summary of the nature, purpose and management of science teaching throughout the school. Much of this is now defined by the National Curriculum Order but will almost certainly need relating to the special circumstances of your school. A school policy statement for science needs to be no longer than two hundred words as it is a statement of intent. This leads to an action plan showing how the intentions will be achieved. The action plan is likely to have four components:

- general aims derived from the policy statement;
- an objective description of the present position regarding science throughout the school;
- a statement of needs and deficiencies; and,
- short- and long-term targets to satisfy these needs and deficiencies.

Progress is helped and considerable time is saved if the science coordinator prepares and presents drafts for each stage to the staff for discussion. You should review the policy statement and action plan regularly to check on progress and, if necessary, revise them. Chapter 12 provides details, with examples, of how you can write a policy statement for science and develop the action plan from it.

A scheme of work is not a part of the policy statement; it is a consequence of it — one of the actions. It is the map your colleagues will use to achieve the aims of science education as identified in the policy statement and action plan. Since each teacher will take the children in a class along only part of the journey, an important task for you as the coordinator is to ensure that every teacher knows where they are starting and what the destination is. It is important that the teacher takes the children to explore new territory and use their earlier experiences in new and different ways rather than simply reiterating them. Again, it helps if you draft a skeleton programme for the staff to discuss and develop. In such a discussion, you will need to bear in mind that the science experiences planned should be checked against the criteria for good practice in science education identified in *Science 5 to 16: A Statement of Policy* (DES, 1985), that is:

Breadth	Differentiation
Balance	Equal Opportunities
Continuity	Varied Teaching Methods
Progression	Links Across the Curriculum
Relevance	Assessment

While recognising that there is no single right way to teach and allowing individual teachers as much freedom as possible in the content and approaches selected, the coordinator has to ensure that the requirements of the National Curriculum Order for Science are satisfied throughout the school. The support of the headteacher in this respect is important, and you will need to work closely with the head to ensure that all develops and runs smoothly and efficiently.

As coordinator, you will soon have to shift from asking *Are all the children receiving good opportunities to learn in science*? to the more evaluative question, *Are all the children learning*? This question can only be answered by comparing aims and targets with outcomes and effectiveness measures. Such evaluation is probably done regularly and informally by

Suggestion

You might find it useful to begin a file in which to record your experiences as the science coordinator. You could use file dividers to subdivide it into sections reflecting the different aspects of your role. Include a copy of your job description which would provide a reference point for these different aspects. Note details of discussions, with dates, and minutes of meetings. Also include programmes for action, copies of policy documents, plans for in-service activities and details of how and when you worked with colleagues in different ways. Other sections would cover budget, resources, liaison and so on.

each teacher. Nevertheless, aims have a tendency to drift and judgments may become unclear and variable. Your role becomes one of evaluation, evidence collection and moderation and will involve developing an overview of each class's progress in science with records which allow you to identify each child's attainments. This process will also enable you to identify where future support and development would be useful. A lot can be learned from displays of children's work, teacher-produced worksheets and workcards, and general comments in the staffroom. More formal assessments help to complete the picture. For the purposes of the National Curriculum, some formal records of teachers' assessments must be maintained. This requires agreed ways of assessing, recording and reporting progress and it is likely that you will have to integrate science into the school's system or devise such a system for science. This is discussed in Part 4.

Thinking about your own professional development

Many aspects of the science coordinator's role can take time to achieve, especially if you are not only new to the role but also new to the school. It is important that you recognise that you cannot do everything at once. Nor will you achieve the success you would prefer with everything that you attempt. Furthermore, while you are busy doing your best for the school and for your colleagues, you must also remember to think about your own professional development and needs.

Like any creative activity, there will be sustained periods of routine effort in order to achieve something worthwhile at the end. Routine effort can be minimised by:
- working out a programme for yourself in your role as the science coordinator;
- seeking advice, when appropriate, from people like your headteacher and your LEA science adviser;
- working cooperatively with other coordinators in your school;
- establishing contact with science coordinators in other schools; and,

■ consulting journals and books where much of the routine work has been done for you.

We will discuss matters related to your professional development in the next chapter.

Summing up

In this chapter we have outlined the two main dimensions of your role as a science coordinator. You will first be a source of support, maintaining the status quo and keeping science teaching going. You will also, and at the same time, be planning and promoting the development of effective teaching and learning in science by starting from current practices and moving forward. Some difficulties you might anticipate and plan for are:
■ ambiguity in your role and the need to have your brief clearly defined;
■ the need to pace changes realistically so that progress can be achieved.

The different aspects of your role will be discussed in the subsequent chapters and some possible solutions will be described. The next chapter will begin by looking at some of the things you need to think about in relation to your own development as a science coordinator.

Chapter 2

Your own development as a science coordinator

Introduction

As part of the government's review of the continuing professional development of teachers, a new national professional qualification for subject leaders (NPQSL) in primary schools is being introduced (TTA, 1996). The consultation document makes clear the standards of skill, knowledge and understanding that are expected of anyone fulfilling this role. These criteria will identify what will be expected of you as the science coordinator in your school and should also support you in identifying your own training needs and development targets.

The TTA (1996) draft standards for subject coordinators in primary schools are in four main sections:
- The coordinator's core role in the school.
- The main areas for development and assessment:
  a) teaching, learning and curriculum;
  b) monitoring, evaluating and improving;
  c) people and relationships;
  d) resource management; and,
  e) accountability.
- The coordinator's own professional knowledge and understanding.
- The coordinator's own skills and abilities.

In later chapters of this book, we attempt to show you how you can approach some of these. Here, we discuss how you can work on your role and also monitor and advance your own development. These are the focus of this chapter.

When you first become a science coordinator, you are likely to feel that you have to make progress quickly. However, be cautious. You can waste a lot of time by not doing the ground work first. In the same way that it is unreasonable to expect you to know everything that there is to know about science and science education, it is also unreasonable to expect you to do everything immediately. You need to plan your work as a coordinator and this will go side by side with your professional development. If you are new to the role or new to the school, the headteacher may have different expectations of you to what she or he would expect of an established member of staff or someone who has been a science coordinator before. Consequently, you need to identify where you are in this scheme of things. There are essentially four stages to your role:

■ *Preparation*
■ *Getting Started*: the new coordinator
■ *Keeping Going*: as you gain experience
■ *Moving On*: developing yourself and moving the school on.

The diagram in Figure 2.1 summarises what might be expected of you at each of these stages.

Monitoring your own needs

There will be a need for you, as the coordinator, to carry out an audit of your colleagues' understanding of science and science education. In a similar way, you will need to audit your own needs as a coordinator. If you have been appointed to the post of a science coordinator, then you are already likely to be a confident and successful teacher, but in terms of your own development the question is, *How can I develop further?* Think about the third and fourth aspect of the TTA criteria.

FIG 2.1
Your developing role as a science coordinator

Preparation:
- Background reading
- Collecting research papers
- Attending courses
- Talking with other coordinators
- Clarifying the role

As a new coordinator:
- Exhibit good practice in your own classroom
- Create attractive displays around the school
- Find out about the resources in the school
- Explore the local environment as a resource
- Begin to pass on information to colleagues
- Talk to colleagues about what they do
- Discuss your role with the headteacher

As you gain experience:
- Organising, managing and replacing resources
- Working with colleagues in their classrooms
- Monitoring and reviewing existing policy
- Liaison with others: governors, parents, teachers in other schools
- Providing training and support through staff development sessions
- Monitoring teaching and learning in science across the school
- Collecting evidence of progress and achievement

Developing yourself and moving the school on:
- Reviewing, revising, rewriting science policy statement
- Restructuring science programmes/schemes
- Progress review and comparisons with national standards
- Looking at more effective strategies (e.g. equal opportunities, differentiation)
- Self-audit of professional knowledge and understanding
- Self-audit of personal skills and attitudes
- Developing your personal action plan
- Updating your own skills, knowledge and understanding

The third related to your own professional knowledge and understanding which, of necessity, must be maintained at a high level. The fourth related to your personal skills and abilities to work with and manage others. In both cases, you should carry out a self-audit at regular intervals, perhaps once a year. An example of a self-audit sheet you could use

FIG 2.2
A self-audit sheet for professional
knowledge and understanding

Audit of Professional Knowledge and Understanding

Carry out an audit of your own professional knowledge and understanding.

Ask yourself the following questions:

1. Am I up to date on science and science-related pedagogy and development? ....

2. Do I have a broad understanding of the key issues in science? ....

3. Am I aware of recent, relevant research in science? ....

4. Do I know what national inspection evidence tells us about science education? ....

5. How does the achievement of pupils in my school compare with national standards in science? ....

6. Are the methods I am using to monitor, develop and improve science teaching in my school the most appropriate? ....

7. Do I need to understand more about how children with different needs learn most effectively in science? ....

8. Am I up to date with health and safety requirements? ....

9. Have I a broad overview of where science sits in the curriculum as a whole? ....

10. Have I read all of the recent publications from government and other national bodies? ....

© Falmer Press Ltd

to monitor your professional knowledge and understanding is given in Figure 2.2, and an example for personal skills and abilities is given in Figure 2.3.

For each question on the self-audit sheets, identify whether or not you feel confident in this respect and qualify your response with a supporting sentence. For some of the questions, you are likely to feel happy with your answer and comfortable with your level of skill, knowledge and understanding. However, there will be a few where you will recognise the need for some support and development. You should prioritise these and think of some possible ways forward. Perhaps it needs some time so you can catch up with

FIG 2.3
A self-audit sheet for personal
skills and abilities

Audit of Personal Skills and Abilities

Carry out an audit of your own personal skills and abilities needed
for working with others. Ask yourself the following questions:

1. Do I exhibit clear educational values? ....

2. Can I motivate and inspire others? ....

3. Am I able to resolve difficulties and take decisions? ....

4. Am I flexible and adaptable? ....

5. Do I solve problems and use opportunities? ....

6. Can I both lead and be part of a team? ....

7. Can I develop, implement and evaluate policies? ....

8. Am I an effective communicator? ....

9. Have I a grasp of management, educational and research issues
   relevant to the school? ....

10. Do I know and use various management strategies? ....

11. Am I sensitive to people and their needs? ....

12. Have I the skills to interpret and use relevant data? ....

13. Do I recognise my own needs and seek support when
    necessary? ....

14. Can I prioritise and manage my time? ....

15. Am I able to use IT, both in science and in management? ....

© Falmer Press Ltd.

---

reading. Alternatively, there may be a course or conference, either locally or nationally, which would help. As well as looking for courses which focus on science, remember to consider more generic ones, such as time management and assertiveness training, which may be of use to you.

Once you have worked out your needs and solutions, discuss the results with your headteacher. He or she is crucial in the process of initiating and continuing your professional development as a coordinator. It is part of his or her responsibility to ensure that you receive the necessary support and training to carry out your role successfully. You should be able to negotiate a programme of non-contact time, either with supply cover for your class or perhaps when a student is working with you.

As the coordinator, you need time to:
- read relevant documents and research;
- write policy statements and action plans;
- plan schemes and programmes;
- design support routes for colleagues;
- spend time with colleagues;
- disseminate ideas;
- collect evidence of current practice; and,
- monitor and evaluate teaching and learning.

Prioritise your needs and discuss them with the headteacher.

Summing up

In this chapter we have looked at ways in which you can ease yourself into your role as the science coordinator, and also monitor your own development and professional needs. Some difficulties you might anticipate and plan for include:
- while dealing with other teachers' needs, you ignore your own;
- finding time to refresh and update your ideas.

In the next chapter we will look at aspects of your role which involve working with others in different ways and for different purposes.

Chapter 3   Working with others

Introduction

Many teachers enter the teaching profession because it allows them to build relationships with and help others, particularly children. Being a coordinator extends that dimension to include greater professional interaction with adults. Good, professional relationships with others makes the role of coordinator easier and more satisfying and contributes to more effective teaching and learning.

As the science coordinator, you will need to work with a number of different colleagues in different ways. First, all coordinators usually have to work closely with the headteacher, who has overall responsibility for the teaching and learning going on in the school. Second, you will need to work individually with some of your teacher-colleagues, advising them about the subject content of science and the best ways to teach science. Third, you will need to disseminate information to all colleagues with whom you work, sometimes in writing, sometimes at meetings and occasionally through staff-development sessions. Fourth, you will liaise with others, not only other adults working in your school — students, supply teachers, parents and governors, for example — but also with people from outside, like members of the inspection or advisory service, staff from other schools and tutors from higher education institutions.

Arrange a time to meet with the headteacher to talk through your role. After school is probably better, to ensure quality time and avoid interruptions. You could use the following as a guide to your discussion:

- take along with you a copy of your job description and talk through it to clarify expectations;
- ask about his/her perceptions of the school's current position regarding science;
- ask for copies of any existing documents relating to science;
- plan a rough timetable for carrying out various actions — what are immediate priorities, what can be delayed, and so on;
- identify the budgetary arrangements and how you can access funds for different purposes;
- clarify the procedures you should follow for different eventualities — if you need money for something, time to carry something out, help with dealing with a colleague, and so on;
- discuss your immediate feelings about your own needs as a coordinator; and,
- finish by arranging a regular meeting, perhaps once per half term — this meeting may be fairly brief but it is an important part of your support as coordinator.

In this chapter, we will look at different ways you may find yourself working with these different people.

Working with your headteacher

Even though you have been appointed to a post of responsibility for science, you should not see yourself as working alone. Realistically, you need to work in consultation with your headteacher. Although she or he has delegated to you responsibility for the science curriculum and matters relating to it, your headteacher will still be your 'line manager'. In particular, the headteacher should be your final source of help and advice when you have problems, worries or needs and you have exhausted all other options. On a more regular basis, the headteacher also needs to be kept informed of what is happening in science and how the school's policy is being translated into practice. This will enable him or her to support any new initiatives you may wish to try. If such initiatives involve release time and supply cover, or have other funding implications, then the headteacher needs to be involved from an early stage so that approval from the school governors can be sought.

If you are a newly appointed coordinator or new to the school, the first thing you need to do is to arrange a meeting with your headteacher to clarify your role and plan how you are going to work together. Decide beforehand what you need to talk about and have your questions or points written down. If possible, give the headteacher a copy in advance of the meeting so that she or he can prepare some responses and thus save time. This will have the advantage of making you appear very organised and efficient. During the meeting, try to keep the discussion fairly formal and take notes. Afterwards, if possible, prepare a summary of your discussion and give the headteacher a copy for comments. This will help you to clarify your position and provide you with starting points for your requests for time or money at a later date.

In most schools, you are likely to find that the headteacher is helpful and cooperative in your endeavours to support and improve the quality of teaching and learning in science throughout the school. This is reasonable, since she or he is ultimately responsible to children, parents, governors and inspectors for the overall quality of what is being provided. Within the school development plans, the headteacher must identify each year which area(s) of the curriculum will be focused upon for development. As part of those plans she or he will want to show:

■ how staff development days are to be used;
■ the nature of any audits or evidence to be collected;
■ the need for supply cover (e.g. for a coordinator to work with colleagues or prepare documents); and,
■ what other funds will be needed and used to support staff development.

When the focus is science, then the actual details of the audits to be carried out, the plans for the staff development days and funding needs for different purposes are likely to be your responsibility. Such details will need to be presented by the headteacher to the governors for approval. This does, of course, give the subject a high level of credibility and you, as the coordinator, the maximum opportunity to make progress in developing science. You can also build into the plans how the headteacher will be involved. For example, it is useful for audits to be carried out in his or her name, and for the headteacher to chair meetings and staff development days, even though you may actually be leading them.

Occasionally, you may feel that the headteacher is giving you less support than you need. If this is the case, then you must ask yourself: *Am I being over demanding? Have I already had my fair share of time / money / support for science? Is there a genuine shortage of money and the headteacher would have to respond this way to anyone at this particular time?* If the answer to any of these questions is, *Yes*, then perhaps you would be wise to shelve your idea for the moment and get on with doing what you can in other ways.

However, if your headteacher is not interested at all, find out from other coordinators how they work. If you find that they have the same difficulties, seek advice from the deputy headteacher or an experienced coordinator. Alternatively, advice could be sought from a science adviser or the school's link primary inspector. However, in all cases you would need to handle the discussion diplomatically so that it is not a complaint about the headteacher. Your aim is to improve matters, not make the working relationship more difficult. If all else fails, then your last resort is to do what you can to the best of your abilities within whatever situation you find yourself. There can be no formula for dealing with difficulties of this nature because they are as varied as people.

Working with other coordinators in school

In your school you may well find that most teachers have responsibility for an area of the curriculum. While the actual subject knowledge focus will be different for each area, the actual principles of support and implementation at the classroom level are likely to be more generic. These will cover things like planning, organisation and evaluation of learning, and how to work alongside colleagues. There will also be basic ideas to do with budgets, meetings and in-service provision which can be shared. Once you have talked with the headteacher, you need to talk either formally or informally with other, more experienced coordinators in your school to find out more about how they work. As with the headteacher, if you arrange a formal meeting plan your questions to make effective use of time. Alternatively, a lot can be learned from informal discussions over a cup of tea during lunchtime.

One of the main tasks of any coordinator in a primary school is to support and encourage colleagues in the establishment of classroom conditions conducive to learning by all children. This includes children who are identified as having special educational needs within mainstream classrooms, and the effective management of their learning is likely to be an area where some of your colleagues ask you for advice and support. Wolfendale (1992) warns against seeing special needs as something grafted on to the curriculum for the minority of children, with the special educational needs coordinator as the repository of responsibility as well as expertise. She argues that:

> ❝ . . . the complex web of a child's needs are such that no one teacher can adequately meet them. (p. 7)

To this end, every child's unique needs must be met in the ordinary classroom by all class teachers who are in turn supported by the appropriate coordinators. Wolfendale goes on to say:

> ❝ The planning and management of the curriculum rightly belongs primarily to curriculum and subject specialists. Where 'collective action' comes in is at points when teachers want to plan appropriate learning opportunities for individual children . . . As she or he moves through curriculum stages progress as well as 'sticking points' are likewise identified. (1992, p. 50)

This highlights the need for you, as the science coordinator, to work with the special educational needs coordinator. While you will identify the curriculum stages in science through which *all* children must progress, your colleague can advise on how to approach the 'sticking points'. Between you, you can also think about how to advise and support your colleagues when teaching science to children with special educational needs generally. Wolfendale suggests some starting points might be:

- creating meaningful, relevant learning opportunities;
- choosing appropriate times to use different formal or informal approaches;
- praising appropriately;
- celebrating individual and group success;
- using appropriate language for instruction;
- encouraging cooperative learning; and,
- offering supportive, non-judgmental interaction with each child.

These strategies seem likely to be successful with all children in any curricular experience, not only those with special educational needs in science.

Suggestion

At a staff meeting, ask your colleagues about their perceptions of science based on their earlier experiences. This could be done as a paper exercise in the following way.

- Give each teacher a sheet of A4 paper.
- For each of the following questions, ask them to answer with the first three words they think of in response.
  How do you feel about science as a subject?
  How do you feel about teaching science?
  What developments in school would help you?
  What in-service activities would be useful?
- Collect in their responses, anonymously if preferred, and collate them.
- What do they tell you about your starting point with your colleagues?
- Can their responses be used to begin some planning for your first staff development session?

If you do not have a special educational needs coordinator in your school, find out if there is someone on your staff who has a particular interest in this area and has perhaps been involved in some in-service training. You could perhaps discuss particular ideas with that person. Alternatively, you could contact your local education authority special needs adviser, and arrange a meeting for the same purpose.

Another coordinator who you may need to talk with is the person with responsibility for assessment. In some schools, this may be the headteacher; in others, the assessment policies are managed by the separate subject coordinators. If in your school there is someone with this responsibility, then once again discussion with him or her could save you a lot of time and effort.

Working with other teaching colleagues in school

Most primary teachers are not science specialists. It is only in recent years that science education has been a major component of teacher training programmes. Consequently, many of your colleagues are likely to bring to their science teaching perceptions of science based on what they themselves did in science in secondary school supplemented by experiences gained through the media. Such perceptions can influence the kind of experiences they provide and what they expect of their pupils.

The mere existence of the National Curriculum Order for Science does not guarantee a sound science education. For example, a teacher's assessment of attainment in science will be in accord with what is seen as the aims of science education. In the teacher's view, the children may have attained appropriate levels of various targets but they may not be the same targets as those of other teachers even though they use the same name. This is one of the challenges facing you as the science coordinator. One of your first tasks must be to find out what the starting point is with each of your colleagues. Only by doing so can you begin to plan how you can support them and help to develop their expertise.

FIG 3.1
Example of a staff audit sheet

Developing Science Throughout the School

Name: _____ Class: _____

How many years have you been teaching? _____

Do you have any of the following science qualifications? (Please tick)

[a] 'O' level or equivalent in:
Biology _____
Chemistry _____
Physics _____
Other _____
If other, please specify
_____

[b] 'A' level or equivalent in:
Biology _____
Chemistry _____
Physics _____
Other _____
If other, please specify
_____

[c] Do you have a science subject as the main part of:
a degree: _____ Please give details: _____
an ITT course: _____ Please give details: _____

[d] Have you attended any INSET courses for science? _____
If so please list the courses:
_____
_____

[e] Have you any other interest or expertise relevant to science not
covered in [a] to [d]? _____ If so, please give details:
_____
_____

What do you find easiest about teaching science to your class?
_____
_____

What do you find hardest about teaching science to your class?
_____
_____

What kind of support would you find most useful right now?
_____
_____

What kind of personal development would be helpful to you in the longer term?
_____
_____

Is there anything else about teaching science which you feel is important for helping with your continuing professional development?
_____

© Falmer Press Ltd

Your colleagues' perceptions will give you a rough guide about where to begin. This can be added to the information gathered during your discussions with your headteacher.

A more objective approach is to carry out an audit of staff skills and expertise in science. This would give you a more accurate picture of their strengths and needs, and allow you, with the headteacher, to plan an appropriate staff development programme. This can be done in a number of ways. The easiest is to prepare an audit sheet for your colleagues to complete. The DFE (1992) provided some useful examples for headteachers of how to carry out audits of teachers' general skills. However, they tended to focus on biographical information (like years of service and qualifications) rather than subject specific aspects. As the science coordinator, although you do need to know about a teacher's qualifications and experience relevant to science, you are more concerned with identifying and supporting their science-specific needs. An example of a staff audit sheet is given in Figure 3.1 (p. 36).

If you design your own audit sheet, there are a number of basic principles to bear in mind:
- be sensitive to some teachers' lack of confidence and competence;
- value positive things which can be used as starting points; and,
- avoid asking questions to do with feelings — be factual and objective.

It is a good idea to talk through your draft version with the headteacher, and ask him or her to issue it for you with a brief covering memorandum explaining why it is needed, how it will be used, how the information will be stored and who will have access to it.

Alternatively, and if time allowed, you could talk to colleagues individually to take advantage of the more personal approach. This can be done informally, at lunchtime for example, or in the more formal context of a staff development day. Use an interview sheet, similar to the audit sheet, to guide your questions to ensure you gather the information you need.

You can supplement your information by looking at displays around the school, the resources that are available and how they are used, and talking with children from different classes about their science, for example, when you are on playground duty, although these approaches are much more subjective.

Once the information has been collected in these various ways, your next task will be to synthesise it in order that you can produce a summary report. You need to focus on the key areas of strength within the school and the particular short- and long-term needs of your colleagues. In a small school, this summary can then be taken to a staff meeting for discussion. In a large primary school, it may be easier to arrange for a small working group to do this. In either case the outcome should be a plan of action based on the needs and what you feel is needed to meet those needs. This will be an integral part of the broader school development process and should also feed into your own personal development. Figure 3.2 (p. 39) shows some possible routes for doing this.

When working with your colleagues, there are certain targets to be achieved. These include: positive motivation, self-esteem, confidence, management and control skills, and enhanced subject knowledge and understanding.

Motivating colleagues

For some primary teachers, science may not have been a major part of their professional training and some may have done very little science at secondary school. Their perceptions and feelings can be very mixed and their conceptions of the nature of science and the role of science education may need to be explored. If you are a science specialist, it may be difficult for you to appreciate that other primary teachers do not share your interest in and enthusiasm for science. If you find that intrinsic motivation is not there, then your colleagues' interest and motivation

FIG 3.2
Routes for developing science

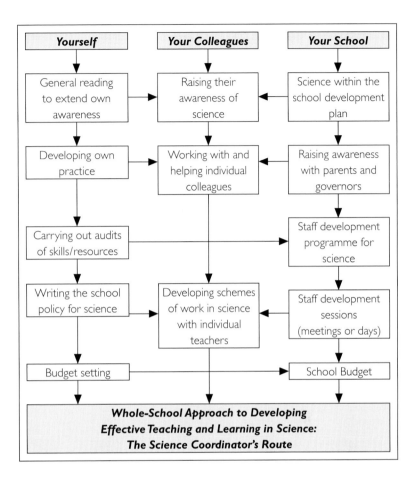

must first be stimulated. This is done by you, as a supportive colleague and member of the team, not as the 'science expert' who is trying to teach them the basic principles of science and telling them what to do. Your aim will be to introduce them to effective and rewarding ways to teach science which draws on their expertise as good primary teachers. One way to do this is by letting them see examples of good practice in your own classroom and working with them on an individual basis.

An alternative approach, useful as a starting point, is to use a short staff meeting, where they can be involved in some activities themselves. Such an approach not only demystifies some of the science, it also allows you to begin discussion about what can be done with children at different ages, what key questions could be asked and explanations given, how the children might record findings, what resources are

Suggestion

Spend half an hour during a staff meeting running a workshop which looks at an aspect of science from everyday starting points. For example:

- *Toys* can be used to introduce ideas related to energy;
- *Kitchen implements* can be used to introduce aspects of forces;
- *Cookery* can help explore ideas about physical and chemical changes.

The task can be subdivided to show how, using starting points drawn from everyday life, aspects of investigation and experimentation and chemical and physical processes are addressed.

needed, how tasks might be differentiated and how the assessment process might be carried out. As when running any meeting, you need to:

- be clear about your aims and outcomes;
- prepare the tasks and related activities carefully;
- circulate beforehand any information which needs to be read;
- organise the room and resources in advance; and,
- leave time for questions and discussion.

During a practical workshop session you can observe colleagues involved in the tasks and you can begin to clarify where individual support might be needed: 'Mrs X knows the science, but is not very good at turning an idea into an investigation. Mr Y is not very good at thinking about different ways of recording, but often explains well.' Such observations can provide the beginning of your plans for a staff support programme.

From the information you have collected and what you have observed, you should then be in a position to prioritise your plans. Ask yourself:

- Where am I starting from?
- Which teacher should I work with first?
- Is it possible to do something with all colleagues?
- How do I build on this?
- What do I need by way of time, money or resources?

Developing teachers' self-confidence and self-esteem

Your next step is to make the teachers feel confident and have a go. It is useful to begin with current successes, share these and build on them. Use in-service sessions or staff meetings to encourage the sharing of experiences that worked well. Choose topics for discussion and ask teachers in advance to talk for a few minutes about something they and their children did which pleased them, perhaps illustrating it with something to show the group. The important thing is to share ideas and show respect for what they already can do well.

Another strategy that can be used to support colleagues is to encourage staff to keep a notebook or diary on science teaching for, say, a few weeks. Teachers could be asked to note their feelings and responses to teaching science as they work. Their comments should include not only their worries, but also the questions they would like answering and the aspects they have enjoyed or found successful. Again, as with perceptions elicited from the earlier activity, these notes can be used by you as the starting point for planning support at a personal level, and also to identify common issues which could be the focus of a staff meeting or an in-service session.

Teachers develop the confidence to try things only when their self-esteem is fairly high and unlikely to be threatened in the process. A part of this is knowing that what they are doing is respected by others and valued.

Managing science activities

The organisation and management of science activities provides inexperienced teachers or those lacking confidence with the most worries, partly because of the potential for behavioural problems. In such cases, they are likely to approach the science coordinator for help. There are a number of alternative approaches to primary science teaching and different ways of organising classrooms for science activities which you might suggest (described in Chapter 12). Ultimately, however, the best way for a teacher to find out what will or will not work is to try them. Most teachers will be happy to do this without support, but one or two might welcome your direct involvement. Initially, the teacher might be released from some teaching by the headteacher to spend a lesson or an afternoon with you, first observing you at work with your class and later working alongside you. This introduces the teacher to various ways of organising and managing different kinds of science activities. Next, following a joint planning session, your headteacher might arrange for you to be released to work with the teacher in his or her classroom. This could involve team-teaching initially, then you withdrawing your involvement until the teacher is working alone. This can be followed by your support with subsequent planning and advice on matters like assessment and differentiation.

Providing classroom-based and school-based INSET

In-service support for teachers can help them to know what constitutes effective science teaching. It is often the coordinator's task to discuss professional development needs with individuals and then plan and support them appropriately. It is also useful to see if the headteacher will be involved in support programmes of this nature so that they are kept informed and might contribute to the process.

Some matters which are common to all staff may be better addressed through staff in-service sessions, either after lessons end, during a staff meeting or on specific staff development days. Unlike working with colleagues on an individual basis, INSET sessions can be quite stressful, since you put yourself on show before all your colleagues. However, although you may be responsible for planning an INSET session, this does not mean you have to provide the input on that day. You may wish to use outside expertise. This is particularly appropriate if you are leading a whole-day session. Since the school will inevitably have to pay your visitor, you must ensure you get value for money. With small schools, it is sometimes useful to plan your INSET work with one or two science coordinators from other local primary schools, so that you can share the costs. Unless the person is booked for the whole day, it is best to use a guest speaker in the morning. This is not only when the staff are fresher and more likely to ask questions, it also provides time for questions and discussion of the speaker which can spread over lunchtime — most speakers will be willing to stay for a free lunch.

Whether you are providing the input on the INSET session yourself, or leading the day, there are a number of things you need to do to ensure it runs smoothly.
- have a clear purpose for the session, with specific aims and outcomes;
- plan for a mixture of types of input and involvement;

If you are wanting to use an outside speaker, there are a number of things you should do:

- talk to other science coordinators or the science adviser about possible speakers, unless you know someone from personal experience who you wish to use;
- identify clearly your aims for the session and what you want from it for your colleagues — make this clear to the speaker;
- check on all costs involved, including travel and copying of materials, and ask for a quotation in writing before you book;
- check with the headteacher that the budget will cover the costs;
- send the speaker a copy of the timetable for the day which includes a confirmation of the agreed payment, and asks for confirmation of any resources needed;
- remember that the more speakers you want to use in one session, the more difficult it will be to find a common date — one or two are best, and avoid overloading your colleagues with information.

- choose a room to work in which is attractive and comfortable;
- prepare textual materials beforehand to minimise note-taking;
- check the numbers involved and the catering arrangements;
- produce a programme for the session and distribute in advance;
- circulate a list of things you wish your colleagues to do beforehand and/or bring with them;
- leave time at the end of the session for general discussion; and,
- evaluate the session by preparing a simple evaluation sheet.

There are a number of sources of ideas for running INSET sessions with staff, designed specifically for curriculum leaders to use. Harlen et al. (1990) have prepared *Progress in Primary Science*. This is a modular programme, each module focusing on a different aspect of science education. The modules cover matters like developing process skills, assessing knowledge and understanding, children's recording skills and continuity and progression. Each module is in two parts: clear guidelines for the course leader and activities for teachers to explore issues and develop skills, knowledge and understanding.

Along similar lines is *Science for Curriculum Leaders* by Clayden and Peacock (1994). This is sourcebook of INSET activities organised into units, each of which focuses on a topic of central concern to teachers of primary science, much like those mentioned above. The units offer background information, resource ideas and activities to carry out with teachers.

Finally, professional journals for primary teachers, such as *Questions/QMS* and the Association for Science Education's *Primary Science Review* provide many ideas for and experiences of running such sessions.

Student teachers

Opting into an initial teacher training partnership with a local university is another way in which the science coordinator can indirectly support staff development. Having students in your school involves developing a training and support programme from which their class teachers could also benefit. Nowadays, students spend longer in schools during their training and the practising teachers take greater responsibility for developing competencies, monitoring progress and assessing them.

In most primary schools, the general mentoring role is likely to fall on the student's class teacher but subject coordinators have an important part to play. You may find yourself in the role of subject mentor. This can involve:

- discussing the school's science policy with students;
- outlining the school's approach to teaching science and how the policy is implemented;
- showing students the range of resources available for their use in science and explaining how they are accessed;
- exemplifying the assessment and record keeping procedures for science and the expectations on students;
- with a class teacher, planning an induction programme to enable students to observe and participate in a range of science activities and lessons across the school;
- supporting them in planning science for a class;
- providing opportunities to discuss and evaluate students' science teaching;
- assessing the students' practical teaching skills in science.

Many schools have a written policy for working with students and you would need to operate within this framework.

Specialist teacher assistants

Some primary schools have STAs — specialist teacher assistants — particularly in Key Stage 1 classrooms. Funding has been provided over the last few years for the training of STAs, usually in a way which involves extensive work in schools alongside teachers. Once trained, STAs can be employed alongside other auxiliary staff in the school on a part-time or full-time basis. The training teaches them about education generally and the primary school curriculum in particular. They are introduced to aspects of teaching and learning, especially as it applies to the teaching of English and mathematics. Some schools are also finding these STAs useful for supporting science teaching and learning, particularly where practical activity is involved. In terms of expertise they seem to fall midway between a qualified teacher and a parent helping out in the classroom, since their training and qualification enables them to be more involved in the teaching and learning process and take greater responsibility than a parent could. STA training is viewed by many as a way of gaining experience prior to training as teachers.

Working with other adults in school

The adult community of the school includes more than the teaching staff. Caretaker and cleaners, dining hall and canteen staff, and the adults who supervise in the playground are all part of the school's community and contribute to it in significant ways. It is a matter of self-interest for you as the science coordinator to build good relationships with such colleagues, since access to the school kitchen provides somewhere to make ice balloons and ice cubes and the caretaker can often provide odds and ends like sand and sawdust for practical investigations.

There are also other adults who may be involved in school activities. These ancillary helpers may not be involved to their greatest effect by teachers. Parents and grandparents, local volunteers who are simply interested in helping out, young people on work experience programmes — all can have valuable skills which, if used carefully, can be a valuable asset. Teachers who use other adults in their classrooms recognise the valuable support they can provide and see them as more than another pair of hands. More schools are involving adults in this way, and many have information packs to clarify expectations and roles. As the coordinator, you may be asked to write some guidelines for teachers on how to work with parents and other adults in the context of science, with safety particularly in mind.

Clear expectations of roles are crucial as one of the difficulties of involving other adults in the classroom is that they may not have a clear idea of what they are expected to do and whether or not they are of any real help. A description of the role of helpers in the school provides not only a helpful framework for what they may and may not do, but also a clear statement of their responsibilities once they have committed themselves to such involvement. To be of real help, such people must be able to give reliable support on a regular basis. This does not mean that they have to commit themselves to every Friday for the school year, although those who can do so would be very welcome. What is involved is for the school to identify a number of people who can support its activities in different ways. Some would be regular, weekly visitors; others might be willing to come in less regularly, but as needed. It is useful to identify who is able to do what and when, and for the headteacher to maintain a list of volunteers in the same way as she or he might keep a list of potential supply teachers for different age ranges of children.

Because science is an area of experience which involves children in practical activity, another adult in the classroom can be advantageous, provided that teacher knows precisely what is wanted from that adult. The involvement needs to be carefully planned and made clear to the helper and some guidance from you may be needed. There are some things which should be clarified beforehand. What is it they are to do? What are the parameters of the task — what can they do and not do? If they are going to be involved with the children in some way, what are the learning targets you want them to focus on? How does this fit in with what has been done previously and what they will be doing next? How should misbehaviour or other non-acceptable responses from the children be dealt with? A notebook, containing summaries of tasks, can be useful.

It is important that the class is prepared for work with a helper, which means letting the children know what is required of them. It also helps to organise a review discussion, perhaps over a cup of coffee at lunchtime, to talk about how things are getting along and what other things are possible.

A programme for the evening might take the following form:

Welcome (by the headteacher — about 5 minutes):
- a brief outline of the purpose of the evening
- introduction of the science coordinator

Introduction (by you — about 10–15 minutes):
- a brief overview of the nature of science and its place in the primary school curriculum
- what science contributes to our children's all-round development
- exemplification of this through the workshop activities

Workshop (hands-on activities — about 30 minutes):
- overall organisation by the science coordinator; each activity/table managed by an individual teacher
- an activity sheet could be used to structure activity and focus attention

Discussion (led by you — about 15 minutes):
- pull the experiences together and tie this in with parents'/governors' prior perceptions of science education and to teaching and learning more generally.

Total time: 1 hour

Tea and a biscuit can be a pleasant way to draw things to a close.

As the science coordinator, you may also need to work with parents and governors. Often, they will not have an extensive knowledge of science. It may be necessary to organise some after-school activities for parents and governors to raise their awareness of primary science education. An open evening with some activities may give them first-hand experience of science. A topic should be chosen in consultation with teaching staff, with each teacher organising a practical activity suitable for his or her class and designed to take no more than a few minutes. This would provide a workshop for parents and governors which would show progression through the topic from the youngest in the school (probably Reception) to the oldest (probably Year 6). Each activity should have clear instructions and questions which emphasise the diverse nature of, for instance, scientific investigation:

> *Explore — How many different ways can you . . . ?*
> *Describe — What do you notice about . . . ?*
> *Predict — What will happen if . . . ?*
> *Investigate — Can you . . . ?*

It might also be appropriate for you to design and duplicate an instruction sheet to guide them through the activities, and possibly on which they could note their responses to the questions.

Involving outside support

There are a number of people and agencies outside the school who can support science teaching, both in school and on visits. They are a resource to be drawn on as needed. One of your tasks as the coordinator is to identify such support and evaluate its potential usefulness. These people and agencies can be matched to topics in the science programme. Some possibilities are:
- emergency services, such as the fire brigade;
- the local vet;
- the local pet shop owner who could bring in animals for a day;
- RSPCA officer;
- RSPB officer;
- local craftspeople.

Visits might be arranged to a local bakery, a garden centre, a supermarket, a churchyard, a building site or a library. More usual places to visit include museums, parks and nature reserves, a zoo, an airport and interactive science centres. Often, museums and science centres have education officers who will come to school to talk to children before or after a visit.

As with other adults working in schools, visitors need to be carefully briefed beforehand. You could help the class teacher plan what is needed and, perhaps, attend the briefing meeting if the visitor makes a preliminary visit to the school. For example, they should be told details of who they will be working with (age, topic, prior experiences, etc.), what is expected of them (talk, demonstration, slides . . .), how the children are likely to respond, and the kinds of follow-up which the teacher will be doing. The teacher will need to ensure that any proposed activities are suitable and safe.

Summing up

In this chapter, we have considered some of the different people you may have to work with in different ways in your role as the science coordinator. These include:
■ your headteacher;
■ your teacher-colleagues;
■ student teachers and STAs;
■ non-teaching adults in school;
■ parents and governors; and,
■ people from outside agencies.

Such a diverse range of contacts will stretch your interpersonal and communication skills, but should give you just as much personal reward as working with the children themselves. Some difficulties you might anticipate and plan for include:
■ finding time to do all you want to do;
■ managing interactions firmly but sensitively; and,
■ persuading colleagues to try new ideas and ways of working without them feeling coerced.

Some solutions have been suggested in this chapter, and we will return to supporting your colleagues' knowledge and understanding in Part 2.

Chapter 4

Contributing to school effectiveness

Introduction

Performance indicators, league tables and accountability make the business of effectiveness high on a school's agenda. It is no longer sufficient for teachers to know that they are effective. They must show this to be the case to the outside world, particularly to parents and OFSTED inspectors.

The effective general management of the school by the headteacher and the management of the separate curriculum areas by subject coordinators is essential for success. This requires you as the science coordinator to:

■ develop the school's science policy;

■ carry out audits of resources and provision;

■ liaise with other relevant people and organisations;

■ run sessions to show others that the science education is effective; and,

■ prepare for inspection.

Developing the school's science policy

The National Curriculum Orders make it clear that the headteacher should:

... consider with his or her staff whether existing schemes of work adequately cover the attainment targets and programmes of study, or, whether the schemes of work need modifying.

(DES, Circular 3/90, 1990)

This is no light task, since it applies to the full National Curriculum. Headteachers are likely to delegate this responsibility to the subject coordinators. With subjects like English and mathematics, the coordinators have a substantial body of experience and resourcing with which to work. Since this is still developing in primary science teaching the task facing you as the science coordinator will be to support a programme of policy development and review to ensure that science stands alongside its core curriculum partners on an equal footing. *Science in the National Curriculum* (DfE, 1995) provides teachers with a framework for developing skills, knowledge and understandings of science. There are now numerous books which provide background science for those primary teachers who need it. Resource books for teachers and commercial schemes also provide ideas for translating the science into classroom experience. However, none of these make a school policy statement for science, nor do they translate the policy into effective classroom practice.

Preparing and reviewing policy

Your starting point is to draw up a programme for policy development and review, of the kind shown in Figure 4.1.

Key elements of a whole school policy for science are:
- a policy statement;
- an action plan;
- a whole-school programme;
- class schemes which focus on skills, knowledge and understanding;
- a strategy for designing lesson/activity plans which focus on teaching approaches and learning targets;
- an assessment, recording and reporting framework, in line with general school policy; and,
- resource management structures.

FIG 4.1
A one-year programme for policy development

	Context: Who is involved? What is the best location?	Focus: How are people involved? What is the aim of this stage in the programme?	End Product: What will be the outcome of this stage in the programme?
TERM 1	[a] Headteacher and science coordinator: HT's room	**Orienting:** to discuss together the current situation regarding science throughout the school; HT and SC to share perceptions; examine existing documents, etc.	**Summary:** of the current situation; list of available resources, funds, etc.; copies of current documentation, if any
	[b] All staff (teaching and auxiliary) plus outside experts: Staff development sessions (half days)	**Focusing:** to provide opportunities for staff to think through and express their views on what science means to them; to enable perceptions to be shared and clarified; to relate views to current educational views and NC requirements; to highlight key issues and principles	**Policy Statement:** succinct summary of the nature of science, the purpose of science education and what staff envisage it has to offer children's education in this particular school, how it fits in with the broader school aims and policies, and a vision of how this will be achieved
		Familiarising: to involve the staff in some experiences to allow them to explore the nature of science and discuss how the NC requirements might be met; to identify individual staff strengths and needs and how these might be met	**Action Plan:** In the light of the above, an outline to show how this will be realised — the current situation; the desired situation; the shortfall
TERM 2	[a] All teaching staff with the help of the SC; possibly LEA advisory teacher involvement: Staff development session	**Organising:** to support staff in translating ideas into practice; to identify relevant contexts and starting points for the science experiences for children of different ages and abilities; to organise effective use of time and resources; to check for breadth, balance, continuity and progression in the skills, knowledge and understanding	**School Science Scheme:** long-term planning in the form of a written statement of the broad scientific experiences planned for the children over a specified time period (for example, the Early Years Unit, a Key Stage or the whole Primary phase)
	[b] Individual teachers in consultation with the SC; Personal planning time directly related to own class teaching	**Planning:** to develop the topics or themes selected for each particular class into achievable targets for teaching and learning; to identify broad general aims and specific goals and targets in relation to the NC requirements for science; to consider the issues of equal opportunities and differentiation; to consider specific resource and organisational needs; to make relevant cross-curricular links	**Topic, Lesson and Activity Plans:** the intermediate and short-term plans produced by individual teachers for their particular classes, outlining the programme for a limited period of time (for example, a half term) and the details on a lesson-by-lesson basis; the latter include specific learning and behavioural targets, teaching methods and organisational strategies, resource needs and curriculum links
TERM 3	[a] Individual teachers with support from the SC; Personal planning time ↓ (Trial of planning and evaluation during this term) ↓ [b] All teaching staff; Staff development session	**Implementing:** to identify the teacher's role during the lesson/activity; to monitor children in appropriate ways as they work for the purposes of assessment; to be available for interaction (discussion, questioning, etc.) as needed; to support in appropriate ways; to maintain records of experiences planned and offered and the learning achieved **Evaluating:** to reflect upon the planning and what was achieved; to use this in future planning to enhance effectiveness	**Lesson/Activity Delivery:** putting the planning into action with associated processes such as assessment of pupils' progress and achievement, record keeping, and evaluation of outcomes **Appraisal:** of the overall programme for fine tuning; policy review and subsequent action planning

Although the context here is science, this is of course equally applicable to any area of the curriculum. Planning, developing and reviewing a school science policy will be discussed in more detail in Chapters 9 and 10, where examples are included. The remainder of this section will focus on the more general principles related to school effectiveness.

A programme for policy development

There are a number of fundamental principles which should guide your actions in designing a programme for developing the school policy for science. The first is that it must be in accord with and build upon the existing more general policies such as those for assessment and school management. Second, it needs to incorporate the broad teaching and learning strategies and approaches favoured in the school, the organisation of space, time and resources and whatever general and specialist help and support is available without at the same time compromising the specific aims of science teaching. The final principle is that the teaching staff should be involved in the development of a policy statement for science. Through it, teachers must reach broad agreement about how to achieve effective science education in the school. The policy statement must be general enough to allow freedom and flexibility within the framework of the National Curriculum Order for Science and specific enough to provide structure, guidance and support for less experienced members of staff.

In order to develop the school policy for science, you will need to guide the staff through a series of stages or processes, identified in Figure 4.1. At each stage, you could ask colleagues a series of questions to encourage discussion.

The kinds of questions you might ask include the following:

Stage 1: Orienting

- What is the staff's current understanding of science?
- What does science mean to them?
- How closely do their perceptions match the rationale which underpins **Science in the National Curriculum**?
- What documents relating to primary science are currently available in school?
- What resources are available in school to support staff?
- What resources (people, as well as physical) are available from outside the school to support staff?
- Is there anything we need to do/buy urgently before we can make a start?

Stage 2: Focusing

- What is the nature of science?
- Why include science in the primary school curriculum?
- What does it offer to our children's physical, social, emotional and intellectual development?
- What are the main aims of science education?

Stage 3: Familiarising

- How much time do the children need to spend on science activities?
- What skills will the children develop and use?
- What knowledge and understanding will be acquired?
- What attitudes will be fostered?
- How can we make the relevance of science explicit?
- What resources will we need?

Stage 4: Organising

- How do we put our ideas into practice?
- Where do we start?
- What contexts are relevant to our school?
- What contexts are appropriate for Reception? . . . for Year 3? . . . for Year 6?
- When is the best time for each class to do science?
- What resources do we already have?
- Where is the best place to store them?
- How should they be stored?
- What resources do we need to collect or buy?
- How can we start planning a whole school programme?
- Which topics or themes are currently used by different teachers?
- What aspects of NC science can be covered by these?
- Is there a balance between the development of investigative science skills and knowledge and understanding?
- What experiences are being unnecessarily repeated?
- What science experiences are being missed out?
- Is any extra work needed at any stage/age to ensure breadth, balance, etc.
- In the light of the answers to these questions, can we now plan a whole school programme for science?

Stage 5: Planning

- What topics or themes will I be doing with my class?
- What will be my broad general aim(s) for each topic?
- What will be my specific learning and behaviour targets for each topic?

- Have I considered the different starting points of the children in my class?
- Have I catered for the different needs and interests?
- Have I referred back to and built upon the children's earlier experiences?
- Have I used opportunities to make relevant links across the curriculum?
- Have I made explicit the relevance of the science in the topic to the children's everyday lives?
- Have I identified assessment opportunities?
- What resources will I need to organise?
- How will the children be grouped or organised?

Stage 6: Implementing

- What will my role, as teacher, be during the lesson?
- Do I know the entry / starting points of the different children?
- Do I have clear expectations of the outcomes?
- What are the key questions I need to ask?
- How will I monitor individuals or groups as they work?

Stage 7: Evaluating

- How do I evaluate progress and achievement?
- How do I record what has been offered / achieved?
- How do I use this information to support children's subsequent learning?
- How do I give feedback on these experiences?
- Where to from here?

Of course, it may be that you are a new science coordinator taking over responsibility for a science policy which is already in place in a school and, further, that the policy is operating effectively. If this is the case, then there is still a need to design a programme for monitoring and reviewing the policy, as indicated above. There is always the danger that policy documents, once written, become cast in concrete.

Since it should be a policy developed by the teachers for the school, it should evolve over time in response to changing needs, new requirements, new opportunities and changes in staff. Policy documents should be viewed as devices to guide effective practices and, as such, they should be subject to revision.

Carrying out audits of resources and provision

An audit is a systematic accounting of something, whether it is money, resources or provision. It serves the purpose of highlighting what is available and identifying what is needed. As such, it is likely to be one of your on-going tasks as a coordinator. An audit will be necessary to gather information when first drawing up a school policy for science. It identifies:

- resources and equipment within the school for teaching science;
- the diversity of teachers' practices in science;
- the assessment and record-keeping procedures;
- how information technology is being used in science; and,
- what textual resources are available for use.

The next step will be to identify shortfalls in resources and provision and plan to rectify them. Not only will you need to consider the financial implications but aspects of safety, and any need for repair and maintenance, as discussed in the previous chapter. Maintaining audit records, ideally on computer which makes them easy to amend and update, is also likely to be part of your job.

Liaison

One of the most significant events in a child's life is when he or she moves from one school to another. For most children, this usually happens when they come to the end of a phase in their schooling, as when they move from an infant to a junior school, from a first to a middle school or from a primary to a secondary school. Whatever the organisational system, there needs to be a smooth transition. Liaison between schools is important and often occurs between the headteachers and also between subject coordinators.

Research indicates that over half the children have mixed feelings about changing schools (Jarman, 1984). On the one hand they are sad to be leaving their old school; on the other, they look forward to new experiences. About 15 per cent of children — usually the more able, confident and self-assured — are happy about moving and confident in the likelihood of future achievement. However, transition worries a large proportion, and for these children — often the timid and less able — myths and fears about transition can dominate their minds. As the science coordinator, effective liaison between yourself and your science colleagues at the next school can help to alleviate some of the children's fears.

Hawkey (1995) found that children worry about:
- the teachers (e.g. increased number teaching science, stricter discipline, less helpful);
- the facilities (more / more advanced facilities for science, equipment like Bunsen burners and chemicals);
- the curriculum content (more difficult / exciting / challenging); and,
- the teaching and learning methods (active involvement, independence, larger classes, small group work).

Hawkey noticed that children had clear expectations but tended to emphasise differences rather than similarities. He took this as an indication that teachers in primary schools, and particularly the Year 6 teacher and science coordinator, need to emphasise the nature and value of the science they have done. Any liaison activities you can arrange, especially visits, open-evenings and induction days, must stress the similarities and continuities in experiences and value the primary science work as the foundation of secondary school science.

The solution is obvious but not easy. You will need to establish links between schools to enable a two-way flow of information. This means sharing ideas, looking at planning, assessment and record-keeping policies and becoming aware of the children's experiences on either side of the transition. This will help to ensure that the new starters build on their prior educational experiences, are challenged academically and adjust quickly to the new organisational structures. HMI (1989) recommend that schools should establish a joint policy for liaison:

> *There are many factors which are associated with the establishment and maintenance of good curriculum continuity and progression in children's learning. Most significant was a joint policy to which all associated schools contributed and which included agreement about [strategies] . . . To be effective, curriculum continuity both within and between schools requires a clear formulated policy and efficient administrative routines.*
>
> (p. 15)

The strategies HMI suggest to encourage liaison include:
- a programme of regular meetings to review and plan;
- curriculum guidelines which span both the primary and secondary phases;
- procedures for assessing attainment at transfer;
- teaching materials which assist the pupils to assimilate the curriculum of the secondary school;
- comparison of teaching styles and learning experiences;
- the use of specialist skills, expertise and interests of both primary and secondary teachers;
- the joint use of facilities and resources;
- the continuation in the secondary school of a theme or project begun in the primary school; and,
- visits by teachers to each other's schools and classrooms and joint participation in the teaching.

Suggestion

You could use Harlen et al.'s list with your colleagues as a starting point for discussion. Consider:

- how the children's day is organised
- the use of cross-curricular planning
- the teachers' language
- the nature of the textual materials used
- the use of displays
- the match of tasks to individual pupils' needs
- the teaching styles used
- the equipment used for science
- the use of homework
- the schemes of work for science
- the recording methods used by pupils
- opportunities given for open-ended investigations

To begin discussion about an inter-school science policy, Harlen et al. (1990) suggest a range of tasks to be completed by a group of teachers from the various schools concerned with liaison. One of the tasks requires comparison of materials and activities in the different schools involved, to consider the similarities and differences between primary and secondary schools.

In the primary classroom, these will need to be considered by you as the coordinator, in consultation with the final year class teacher to calm children's fears about the real and imagined differences.

Preparing for inspection

When inspectors visit schools, one of the indicators of effectiveness they will look for is the effective use of resources. Coordinators are just as much a resource for the school as are teaching materials and equipment. The school development plan should indicate how human resources will be used. The plan will need to indicate how you, as the science coordinator, can become established and develop in your role. As such, during an inspection it is quite likely that the inspectors will review the job descriptions of coordinators and will ask to talk to those holding particular curricular responsibilities. You should, therefore, be prepared for this.

Having our professional practices monitored and inspected can be stressful. We may be aware of our own strengths and weaknesses and inspections seem to make the latter loom large. An inspection is usually a very formal affair, involving a lot of documentation. It is important that the paperwork gives a clear picture of policy and provision in science education and that this is reflected in actual teaching practices.

In addition to the pressures associated with preparing your own class and classroom for inspection, you must also carry a great deal of responsibility for the science curriculum.

There are a number of things to do to show science education at its best. The message you will want to give should show:

- that everyone in the school is committed to high quality science education;
- that teachers are working as a team towards a whole school approach which focuses upon where the children are coming from and where they are going to in their scientific development;
- that all staff were involved in policy development and planning implementation through action plans;
- that there is consistency in policy development, interpretation and implementation across curricular areas and throughout the school;
- that long-, medium- and short-term planning is firmly in place, with sufficient detail and clarity and tight monitoring;
- that the planning encompasses not only curriculum details but also details of organisation and approaches, assessment, record keeping and reporting to relevant audiences;
- that a quality assurance programme is in place which incorporates monitoring, review and development of the science education in the school on a regular basis (perhaps focusing upon one core curriculum area per year);
- that there is a programme for efficient budgeting which takes into account action plans and needs;
- that various partnership programmes are in place to encourage productive involvement with different organisations and groups for the benefit of the children, for example, a home–school links programme; initial teacher training partnership arrangements with local universities; links with local businesses and industries;
- that other beneficial initiatives are in place, for example, the school's use by the community; establishing a nature reserve; etc.

Summing up

In this chapter we have discussed how you, in your role as the science coordinator, will help to contribute to the overall effectiveness of your school. This contribution will be focused upon the development of the school's policy for science and all that that entails. You will also be involved with audit procedures, with liaison with colleagues from other institutions, and with quality assurance procedures like school inspection. Some difficulties which you might anticipate and plan for include:

- finding time to draft, finalise and review documents;
- carrying out audits of current practices and procedures; and,
- establishing links with other schools to facilitate continuity.

Some suggestions have been made in this chapter. Others will be discussed in more detail in later chapters.

Part two

What science coordinators need to know

Chapter 5   Interpreting the National Curriculum

Introduction

The curriculum thought to be appropriate for children of school age inevitably changes over time as different skills, competencies and areas of knowledge are valued. In England and Wales, the Education Reform Act of 1988 provided for schools a formal curriculum policy and identified what is currently deemed essential for all pupils between the ages of five and sixteen. This formal curriculum is also embedded in a broader framework of the whole curriculum, which recognises the importance of cross-curricular dimensions, themes and skills, especially at the primary school stage. What the Education Reform Act did not specify was how schools were to interpret and implement this curriculum policy, although guidance was given in various National Curriculum Council documents. This process was left to the staff of the schools themselves which, in reality, means to the headteacher and subject coordinators. As the science coordinator, you will be expected to be involved in this process for the National Curriculum Order for Science. This means thinking about and helping your colleagues to understand and interpret what science is all about, so that they can be in a strong position to implement science effectively in their classrooms.

This chapter will discuss what science is all about and how its different aspects underpin the National Curriculum Order for Science. It will also describe some ways in which you can help your colleagues to understand its nature and relevance.

What science is all about

The scientific enterprise can be seen as having three major aspects which teachers of primary science will need to understand and address in some way (Newton, 1989).

■ Science is a *product* — a body of knowledge which requires understanding facts, laws, principles and generalisations;

■ Science is a *process* — a way of thinking and working which requires the development and practice of skills;

■ Science involves *people* — it is of direct relevance to all our lives and this relevance needs to be made explicit.

When the Association for Science Education launched its professional journal for primary teachers in September 1986, it provided a statement of policy for teaching primary science which captured the essence of these different facets.

> *Primary science is best seen as a practical activity which makes use of first hand experience to begin the development of skills and concepts of science. It should start to lay the foundation of knowledge and understanding whereby children may develop confidence within a scientific and technological society, and become capable of reflective and adaptive thinking, planning and decision making.*
>
> (*Primary Science Review*, **1**, p. 18)

One of your tasks as the science coordinator will be to ensure that these three facets of science have a part in the experiences offered to the children in your school. Each of them is considered in turn in this chapter.

Science as a product

One of the major aims of science teaching is to help children to understand the natural world in which they live. This is not easy to achieve, since teachers cannot simply give children understanding. It is something learners have to build or construct for themselves. What teachers can do is use a range of strategies to support children as they construct their understanding of the scientific world. They can do this most effectively if they, themselves, understand the main ideas of science they have to teach. A major role for you as science coordinator will be to support your colleagues in developing and extending their own conceptual knowledge and understanding of science where necessary. You will also need to enhance their awareness of how children learn science and the range of strategies they can use to support children's understanding.

Teachers' understanding of science

Teachers will need to match the learning experiences offered to children with what is judged to be appropriate to the children's needs, abilities and interests, all within the framework of the science curriculum itself. The importance of such a match, and the lack of it in practice was described by HMI (DES, 1978) and reiterated in the National Curriculum Council's (NCC) Non-statutory Guidance for Science (1989):

> *Providing appropriate learning experiences ... requires care-ful planning and sensitive teaching by teachers with a broad understanding of science and the ability to match the work to their pupils' capabilities. Activities must challenge all pupils and, at the same time, provide them all with success at some meaningful level.* (NCC, 1989, p. A9)

The question of teachers' own scientific knowledge and understanding was, according to Harlen (1991), brought to the top of the science education agenda by the implementation of the National Curriculum. She considered that,

> *The problem noted by HMI in 1978 as 'the most severe obsta-cle to improvement of science in primary schools' can no longer be set aside.* (p. 20)

Some of the teachers you will work with as a coordinator will have little science in their backgrounds. An emphasis on learning the facts of science may make less demand on them since these may appear relatively easy for the non-scientist to teach. However, if the emphasis is on developing the learner's conceptual understanding and an active involvement in scientific investigation to develop procedural understanding, then the deeper and more comprehensive these teachers' own knowledge and understanding of science, the better. If teachers are unsure about science and lack confidence in their abilities to teach it, how can they judge what is necessary and appropriate for the children? Your guidance and support as science coordinator will be crucial in this respect. Certainly, HMI reports on the early years of National Curriculum Science point to weaknesses in primary teachers' own knowledge of science and the shortage of well-trained and knowledgable science coordinators to support them (HMI, 1991; HMI, 1993). Supporting teachers as they develop their own scientific knowledge and understanding is likely to be one of your more demanding tasks.

Children's learning in science

Children do not come to a classroom with empty heads. They can have many ideas about many science topics and these have been developing from a very early age. These ideas are based on their direct experience of the world around them and also on the ideas they collect from others — family, friends, television and books. They may not be truly scientific ideas but they can serve that purpose and be just as acceptable to the children. They use them to make things make sense. Some of these ideas, even if partially or totally incorrect, can be very difficult to change. Children can be tenacious in their hold on these ideas, even when faced with contrary evidence. This means that learning involves developing and changing existing ideas, but simply telling children things does not necessarily mean the children will understand. New ideas must link meaningfully with existing knowledge and be preferred in thinking about things. You will need to support teachers in understanding what changes, how it can be changed, and how they can plan for such changes to take place.

Strategies which support understanding

The range of strategies available to support the development of understanding is wide but not necessarily well known to all teachers.

As the coordinator, you need to encourage your colleagues to think about the strategies they use. There are a number of strategies that you can introduce that will help teachers support children in the construction of understanding in science. They include:

- using examples;
- using analogy and metaphor;
- using discussion and questioning;
- using contrary experiences; and,
- using problem-solving investigations.

Bridging with examples

Here, a teacher bridges from the known to the unknown with examples. Suppose, for instance, we want to explain evaporation. The teacher might begin with a hot, steaming pudding and show water condensing on a nearby cold plate. A hot, damp tea towel shows the same effect near a cold window. On the washing line, this still goes on but we may not be able to see it.

Bridging with analogy and metaphor

This is the same as the above strategy but makes use of analogy and metaphor to parallel what is to be learned. For example, when teaching about living things and environments, the analogy might be made that the birds in the air are like fish swimming in water and they (the children) walking on land are like the crabs walking on the sea-bed. When teaching about the reflection of a light ray from a mirror, the analogy to a billiard or snooker ball bouncing from the side cushion might be used.

Using questioning and discussion

Lasting understanding builds on existing knowledge and understanding and extends it through new experiences. Discussion and the use of focused questions help to draw out children's prior knowledge and allows the teacher to check what science understandings the children already have. Teachers are very good at using questions to encourage children to recall and describe knowledge and procedures. Research shows the abundance of descriptive (*What . . . ? When . . . ?*) and procedural (*How . . . ? Who . . . ? Where . . . ?*) questions which teachers ask in science lessons. However, teachers seldom push the children beyond recall and description of facts and procedures. To support the construction of understanding, questions need to be asked which force the children to predict (*What will happen if . . . ?*), explain (*Why do you think . . . ?*) and apply (*Can you . . . ? Does . . . ?*).

Requiring children to explain their ideas to others — their classmates or their teacher — and apply them in new contexts can support the process of constructing understanding. Such explanations can be oral, pictorial or written.

Using contrary experiences

Applying what they know in new contexts will sometimes be difficult for children. This is hardly surprising, since when involved in new experiences they are likely to have only a tenuous grip on the new understanding they are constructing and that same understanding is likely to be closely tied to the context in which it is being experienced and acquired. The teacher can help to focus on what is relevant by using the earlier strategies mentioned — for example, analogy and discussion with focusing questions. This refocusing support can help the children to broaden their somewhat limited experience and see how the ideas they have acquired can be applied in different contexts and under different circumstances. It also allows for misconceptions to be brought out and to be challenged. The strategy which

Strategies to support understanding is a good theme for a staff development session. Trying some for themselves can help teachers appreciate the problems the children have. Ask your colleagues the following question:

■ What does 'supporting understanding in science' mean to you?

You could then make a short presentation to illustrate the range of strategies possible, and involve them in a brief discussion by asking them:

■ Which strategies do you use to support the development of understanding in your own classroom?
■ Which strategy(ies) do you think were the most effective? Why?

Finally, involve teachers in a collaborative activity in which they think of examples of the different strategies for selected topics, perhaps focusing on what those teachers will be doing with their classes the following half term.

supports this is one of confrontation by contrary experience. For example, during the discussion about producers and reflectors of light, one child is convinced that crystals produce light. Confront his idea by sending him into a store cupboard with a crystal. Can he see by its light?

It can sometimes be difficult to think of contrary experiences for children which are feasible in the primary classroom. As the science coordinator, you may even have difficulty with some misconceptions held by your colleagues. For example, it is difficult to take to the limit a person's misconception that if water is deep enough anything will float. This particular misconception is a real one which we have experienced with primary teachers. In such events, the explanation has to be applied in as many and varied situations as possible, with the learner predicting what will happen. The process of changing and replacing conceptions can be a slow one. We tried beakers, buckets and a large aquarium to no avail. The local river was the next step!

Using problem-solving investigations

Practical investigations, particularly where there are ideas to test or problems to solve, call for active mental as well as physical participation on the part of the children. They can be very effective for building lasting understanding. Their value is in the need to recall and test prior knowledge considered useful for the task. If this fails it has to be adapted or changed and retested. The evidence of a practical situation is hard to argue with. For example, ask children to explain why a circle of light on a wall, produced by shining a torch, shrinks as you move closer to the wall. To solve this problem they need to bring together their previous ideas about how light travels and apply it in a new situation. This is forcing them to make predictions, hypothesise, and test ideas. This last strategy is, of course, closely related to the second facet of science, science as a process.

Science as a process

Science involves more than knowing scientific ideas and using that knowledge to describe and explain situations and events in the world around us. It is also an active mental and physical process of gathering, extending and reworking that knowledge base. Science is a process — a way of thinking and working. Old and new ideas are discussed and may be tested to see whether or not 'they hold water'. A second aim of science teaching is to introduce, practise and develop some facility in using the skills and processes involved in scientific exploration and investigation. This is the fundamental aim of Sc1: *Experimental and Investigative Science.*

Science as a process is a source of misunderstanding and confusion for some primary teachers, and as such, it is an aspect of science which again will need your support and exemplification as the science coordinator. Your colleagues will need to plan for and provide children with opportunities to acquire the procedural knowledge and understanding which they can then practise and use in new, investigative contexts. However, skills cannot meaningfully be practised in isolation. Children need something to think about and work with; real contexts in which to apply their skills. In an ideal world, the children would generate these contexts for themselves, according to their particular interests. However, in the world of classroom science, where time is not infinite, these contexts need to relate to the conceptual knowledge base we want children to acquire, in other words the content of Sc2: *Life Processes and Living Things*, Sc3: *Materials and their Properties* and Sc4: *Physical Processes.* You may need to support teachers in their attempts to bring together these aspects in an effective and purposeful way. Chapters 6 and 7 provide some examples of how you can do this.

Science and people

The National Curriculum tends to direct teachers' attention on science as a body of knowledge and as a way of thinking and working, that is, those products and the processes which make science what it is. Quite correctly, this may make teachers think about what scientific ideas children should understand and what they should be able to do. There is a

Suggestion

At a staff meeting, ask colleagues for their perceptions of a scientist. They could sketch a scientist or write a list of the characteristics. Be careful not to cue gender in the instructions you give them. Compare their responses. How many identified the stereotype — male, spectacles, beard, receding hairline, various instruments, white coat?

This can lead to a useful discussion about a school approach to avoiding stereotyping and lead on to thinking about wider issues of relevance and equal opportunities.

third aspect which needs to be considered, the relevance of science for people. It is often easy for teachers to see the relevance of what they teach but it may not be so apparent to children. Relevance needs to be made explicit.

Many primary teachers are good at establishing an immediate relevance. When introducing lessons or topics, they use pictures, artefacts, stories and poems, or visitors to the classroom (human and other animals). The aim is to capture the children's attention and interest and it often works well. This is not the same as the wider and longer term relevance of science education. As a science specialist, a coordinator is likely to be very familiar with such relevance but you may find your non-specialist colleagues less well informed and less effective at making such relevance explicit to children.

How relevance is approached depends on a child's stage of development and experience. With younger children, the things which are most meaningful to them tend to be those which are close to them both physically and emotionally: themselves, their family and friends, their homes and the immediate and local environment. As children get older and gain more experience, they are more able to stand back from situations, empathise with others and travel in their imaginations to more remote situations (see Figure 5.1).

With younger children, activities and situations should enable them to participate actively in the process of science — doing science, working like a scientist on matters related to their immediate, local environment. The children can experience for themselves the satisfaction of 'being a scientist'. The child's awareness can be increased by asking them if they enjoyed it and using the ubiquitous happy-face, self-evaluation sheets. This relevance has the bonus of helping to break down stereotypical images of science and

FIG 5.1
The transition in the wider relevance of science

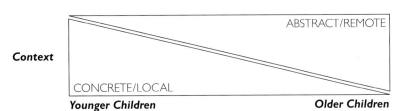

At a staff meeting or staff development session:

1 Ask staff to list two or three topics or themes which they feel are particularly appropriate to different Years in school.

2 For each topic, as a group brainstorm how they might make the relevance of science explicit for that particular age group.

3 Consider the cross-curricular potential of relevance related to each topic.

4 List some starting points from the history of science which might be appropriate with particular classes. Are there any local resources — places to visit, famous people who lived in the area, museums, and so on — which can be used?

the scientist. Images of scientists as male, bald and bearded, with spectacles and a white coat and working alone in a laboratory surrounded by an assortment of chemical apparatus, form very early, before the end of Key Stage 1, and once established can be very difficult to change.

Current events or situations with which the children are familiar can serve as starting points and provide real-world contexts. A new baby can lead to investigating 'Growth and Change'. A supermarket visit can allow 'Materials' or 'Foods' or 'Packaging' to be investigated. Some commercially produced schemes take this approach, providing stories about common events like 'Washing Day' or 'Bonfire Night'. Teacher-designed science trails around the school can also usefully emphasise the impact of science on our lives.

As children mature and gain experience, wider issues should be addressed. Older children at Key Stage 2 can debate the social and moral issues related to the importance of the rainforest or the most recent oil tanker disaster. Children's books, stories and poetry can aid such debate and, as a result of the discussion, ideas for experimentation and investigation can arise on, for example, 'Polluting Our Environment'.

Introducing older children to the history of science by relating the lives of some scientists can help to address some of the stereotypes they hold. Showing them male and female scientists perhaps working out of doors as well as in laboratories, with plants and animals as well as machines and glassware, and in teams may provide alternative role models.

It is usually better not to rely too much on the utility of science (through technology) as a means of pointing out its relevance. Sooner or later, teachers will have to teach something which seems to have little practical utility. Similarly, other subjects may lack practical utility but are still worth doing, so utility must not become the only yardstick of relevance.

Summing up

In this chapter, we have described the different aspects of science which you will need to encourage the teachers in your school to think about when they are planning science, namely products, processes and people. How these relate to the National Curriculum Order has been discussed. Some difficulties you might anticipate and plan for include:

■ teachers' own perceptions of science will influence what they are likely to do in the classroom with children;
■ some staff may hold incomplete or erroneous conceptions of science which you will need to help to change.

Some suggestions you can try for bringing ideas out into the open have been given. In the next chapter, we will look in more detail at supporting teachers' understanding of science as a process.

Chapter 6

Interpreting experimental and investigative science

Introduction

The first attainment target for science, Sc1, is concerned with the mental processes and practical skills which enable children to think and work in a scientific way. Research has suggested that some primary teachers have difficulty with Sc1, so it is likely to be an area where direction and support from you as the coordinator are helpful. For example, in a study of 9- to 11-year-old children and their teachers, Skamp (1986) found that the teachers often included in their lessons activities which involved observing, planning at specific levels within an investigation, and using measuring instruments. Less often seen were opportunities for children to raise questions for investigation, interpret, hypothesise and plan a whole investigation at a more general level. Skamp also noticed that some skills were not used by children at all unless they were directed to do so by their teachers.

A similar picture was found by HMI during evaluation of the implementation of the National Curriculum Order for Science (DES, 1991). The report indicated that although many teachers designed activities which used observation, description and communication, fewer provided opportunities to develop prediction, hypothesising, or whole investigations (Newton, 1992).

FIG 6.1
Exploring, experimenting and
investigating in the National
Curriculum

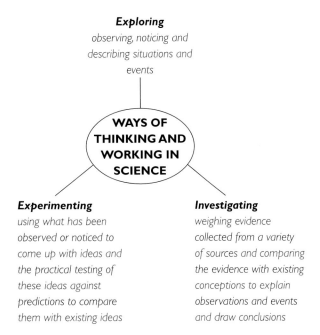

Exploring
observing, noticing and
describing situations and
events

WAYS OF THINKING AND WORKING IN SCIENCE

Experimenting
using what has been
observed or noticed to
come up with ideas and
the practical testing of
these ideas against
predictions to compare
them with existing ideas

Investigating
weighing evidence
collected from a variety
of sources and comparing
the evidence with existing
conceptions to explain
observations and events
and draw conclusions

As the coordinator, you will probably need to define the different skills and processes that constitute Sc1, and clarify the different approaches which can underpin experimental and investigative science.

Aspects of Sc1

Although Sc1 is mainly concerned with *experimentation* and *investigation*, there is a third aspect, *exploration*, which is also important, especially with younger children or when introducing new or difficult ideas. Although the three are distinct, they also closely interrelated (see Figure 6.1).

In the National Curriculum, science experimentation and investigation are two different entities. Sometimes you will find that teachers confuse investigative activities with experiments, and also fail to distinguish between exploring and investigating. Investigation has a broader meaning than experimentation. For instance, children might use research skills to collect information about the Solar System from library books. This does not constitute scientific experimentation but is investigation in the sense of an investigative journalist who finds out more about things, and exploration, involving the use of secondary sources and various communication skills. Indeed, there are many kinds of science activity that children might usefully participate in to develop their knowledge and understanding and skills and procedures. However, not all these activities are actual experiments or even investigative activities. Not everything in science can be investigated by children in an experimental way, for example, as with a study of Earth in Space.

At all stages in their science activities discussion between children and their teacher is valuable. Through discussion, questions are raised for investigation, variables are identified and controlled, ideas developed and communicated, and relationships explained. However, it is part of the difficulty that children need experience to draw upon to ask questions, notice, suggest ideas and explain. This highlights the importance of the different kinds of practical activity for different purposes in science. As the coordinator, you may need to reassure teachers that all of these different aspects of science as a process are not only allowable, but are actually important and necessary for effective teaching and learning in science.

The kinds of activity within Sc1

Parallels are often made between scientific investigation and criminal investigation, and this can be an interesting and relevant way to introduce science as a process to your colleagues. Detectives, like Sherlock Holmes, investigated crimes by looking for clues, recording accurately what they noticed or found, sorting out that evidence and interpreting it to reach conclusions. On the surface, scientific investigation in the classroom uses similar skills — observing, predicting, interpreting and concluding. However, the scientific activity which underpins Sc1 is much more than an investigation of a unique event of the kind Sherlock Holmes had to deal with. The development of children's abilities to think and work scientifically requires teachers to provide opportunities through different types of practical activity, each of which achieves different ends and contributes to the whole — ultimately the ability to investigate independently. These activities are designed to develop:

■ fundamental skills;
■ exploration skills;
■ direct experiment skills; and,
■ independent investigation skills.

Any or all of these skills can be focused upon with children at any age and there is no particular order to their introduction.

One possible reason for a neglect of certain processes by some of your colleagues may be a failure to distinguish between these various kinds of activity. Another reason is the temptation for teachers who lack confidence in science to play safe, rather than stretch the children with real prediction, hypothesis testing and scientific explanation. Even when activities are provided, it is too easy for teachers to overestimate the children's starting abilities. One of your tasks as the science coordinator will be to make clear the distinction between the different kinds of activity and the purposes they serve.

Think About:
One of the things as coordinator you will need to watch for is any tendency for teachers to offer children a rich diet of exploration, in the belief that other skills and processes are being developed as well.

You could try asking your colleagues to carry out a self-assessment of the practical activity in their classroom.
■ What type of practical activity is it?
■ What aim or target is it achieving?
■ What specific skills and processes are being practised and developed by the children?
■ What are the outcomes?

Much of this information might be available from the teacher's lesson/activity plans.

An alternative, and more objective, approach would involve you observing the teacher at work, if the headteacher could arrange cover for your own class. A structured observation schedule could then be used.

If you can identify teachers' understanding of Sc1 and what they do, or think they do, you can then make a start on their further development. As you look at teachers' accounts of their practical activity, or observe them at work in the classroom, look for evidence of them providing opportunities for activities which use fundamental skills, exploration, directed activities and independent investigation.

Fundamental skills activities

There are a number of fundamental or basic skills that are not unique to science and yet they are essential for effective investigation. For example, the manipulation of materials, measuring skills, and recording skills. Initially, structured teaching is needed to ensure these skills are developed. On occasions, the teacher will be focusing exclusively on particular skills by providing exercises for this purpose. However, although intended to develop particular skills, they should still relate to some aspect of the National Curriculum. Language and communication skills would fit into this category, and so children need to be given opportunities to record and communicate their ideas and activities in different ways and for different purposes. Similarly, various mathematical skills — measuring and graph work, for example — are useful in science.

Exploration activities

Exploration activities provide direct experience of a scientific phenomenon, property or relationship. Such activities tend to emphasise observation and communication. When children begin school they are already keen observers of what goes on. They can use several senses, not just sight. They can also communicate their observations in a variety of ways. The problem is that such observation and communication can be unfocused and shallow. In science, these skills have to be sharpened and refined so that children can observe, record and communicate for a purpose and with precision. Such skills development can be supported by the use of physical aids, such as hand lenses or binocular microscopes. These practical experiences should be supplemented as appropriate by using other sources, such as pictures, books, television and video materials, computers and educational visits.

Directed experiments

Directed experiments are intended to provide opportunities to find out more about some particular aspect of what has been explored. In the context of something being tested in a fair way, directed experiments bring together a variety of skills, such as manipulating materials, measuring, observing, recording appropriately and communicating ideas. This might be of a highly structured practical activity which is carefully planned and directed by the teacher. With directed activities the teacher has a clear target or outcome in mind. Throughout, the teacher is very much in control of the activity.

One such target might be to introduce the children to the idea of a fair test. The directed experiment set up by the teacher would give the children the opportunity to change one factor. They would then observe and measure the effect of this change on the other factors, which they would be keeping the same. For example, the children might be given a range of materials and asked to find out which material was the best for slowing down how quickly an ice cube melts. They might be asked to find out which surface is best for bouncing a ball.

Independent investigations

Children must also be given opportunities to practise their skills and processes in more open-ended investigations. Children may contribute more to the questions raised for investigation, planning what is to be done, what techniques are to be used, what evidence has to be collected, how to record their findings and how the evidence will be used. For example, following some work on the properties of some common materials the children might be asked to plan and carry out a fair test to investigate which of five different makes of kitchen towel is best for soaking up water. Economic awareness might also be introduced by extending the problem to ask, Which of the five is the best value for money?

FIG 6.2
An example of science skills and processes: A trip to a harbour

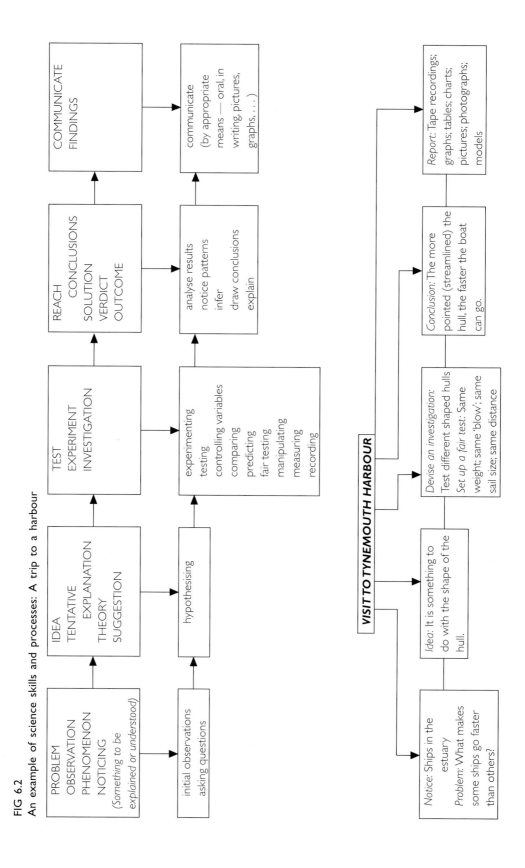

What does scientific investigation involve?

This section summarises briefly the key skills and processes which underpin the four types of practical activity described. The summary is selective but a more detailed account of the skills and processes of Sc1 can be found in, for example, Newton and Newton (1993) which you could use with colleagues during a staff development session.

Teachers can support children's understanding in science by having them investigate situations which highlight the key concepts or ideas we want them to acquire. For example, we provide experiences which involve the children in *observing*, *noticing* and *describing* situations and events. Drawing on their observations and descriptions, the children may then be asked to form an idea to *explain* something and use that explanation to *predict* what will happen next. The idea might then be translated into a *fair test* to see if events go as predicted and *evidence* is collected in the form of results to verify or negate the prediction. The evidence is weighed and some *conclusions* are reached about how good (or otherwise) the idea was that we started with. This is shown in Figure 6.2, which summarises the scientific investigations following from a trip to a harbour.

This sequence of actions is often shown diagrammatically in books on science teaching as the scientific method. It is *a* method rather than *the* method, since it is, of necessity, flexible. Children can observe, notice and predict without having to be involved in a full investigation. Similarly, children may be given data which they did not collect themselves for analysis. Primary teachers are generally good at providing experiences in which the children can observe, notice and describe. Some teachers may, however, encounter difficulties with constructing explanations and translating ideas into predictions and fair tests, and may need your support in this respect.

An activity like the one described above can be a good starting point for you to focus in more detail on Sc1 on a staff development day, since the task can be followed by specific workshop activities requiring prediction, fair testing and so on. The workshop could focus on an area of science content which has been identified by one or more of your colleagues as being problematic.

When children are involved in experimental and investigative science, opportunities for discussion are crucial for developing their ideas, and you should encourage colleagues to make time for children to express and share ideas. Remember to include discussion time in any workshop sessions you plan for the same reason. Discussions need to be as carefully planned and monitored as any other science activity.

Worthwhile explorations and investigations can be difficult to construct, given limited resources and even more limited experiences of primary-aged children. Your colleagues will often approach you expecting ideas more or less for immediate use. To this end, you should devise and search for ideas of this kind. Professional journals are a good source of such ideas. Relate them to the school's scheme for science and particular Key Stages, and file them for ready access.

Summing up

We have described in this chapter the different kinds of activity which constitute experimental and investigative science, and tried to show how each serves a different purpose and has a place at different times in the classroom. Some difficulties you might anticipate and plan for include:
■ your colleagues lack of clarity as to what the different skills and processes in science actually involve;
■ a lack of awareness of the variety of ways practical and investigative activity can be carried out in science.

Some ideas have been provided as to how you can begin to help your colleagues clarify their ideas about Sc1. In the next chapter, we will look at how Sc2, 3 and 4 can provide the vehicle for carrying these skills along and describe a strategy for advising your colleagues on how to do this effectively.

Chapter 7	Interpreting life processes and living things, materials and their properties and physical processes

Introduction

The National Curriculum Order includes science as a body of knowledge. Teachers must help children acquire this knowledge at an appropriate level and with understanding. It is not possible to describe the science which underpins Sc2: *Life and Living Processes*, Sc3: *Materials and their Properties* and Sc4: *Physical Processes* in the space available, nor is it the purpose of this book. If this kind information is needed, coordinators could refer to one of the wide range of textbooks available, or to books like *A Question of Science* (Newton and Newton, 1995).

As the coordinator, you will be aware that knowing the science is not, in itself, sufficient. Teachers must also know how to make that science suitable for children, they must know the way children tend to think, and they must have a range of strategies and approaches for teaching science. Consequently, you will often be asked to help a colleague to plan a lesson, a topic or a sequence of activities in science. You may be approached at any time, not always conveniently so, and you will be expected to respond in a supportive way.

This chapter will outline briefly the main concepts fundamental to science as a body of knowledge and appropriate for primary children. Some of the ideas children have will be discussed and some strategies for changing these ideas and supporting children's construction of understanding will be described. Finally, a strategy for supporting colleagues which can be used by you as the coordinator will be provided.

Some concepts relating to science as a body of knowledge

As the coordinator, you should check that the school programme for science is providing appropriate opportunities for children to acquire the concepts and ideas which underpin the National Curriculum Order. You need to check that these are occurring in at least one Key Stage and possibly being revisited more than once.

Life processes and living things

The experiences that introduce children to ideas about living things in the world around them will often relate directly to the immediate, local environment.

Check:
- Some things are alive, some were once alive and are no longer, and some have never been alive.
- There are a number of life processes common to all living things.
- People are living things and we carry out these life processes.
- Green plants are living things which carry out these processes, too.
- Plants and animals can be classified — sorted into groups — using certain features.
- Plants and animals are found in a range of different habitats.
- Plants and animals are adapted to the environments in which they live.
- Plants and animals depend upon one another and the non-living environment in which they live.

Materials and their properties

The experiences offered to children to introduce them to *materials* usually begins with those that are in their immediate environment. They include activities to show how changes affect materials and can lead to work on solids, liquids and gases and making and separating mixtures.

Check:
- Materials in our environment show great variety.
- Different materials may have different properties, which enable them to be used for different purposes.
- Materials can be grouped in different ways according to their properties.
- In general, a substance can be classified as a solid, a liquid or a gas.
- There are differences in the ways substances behave when they are in these different states.
- Substances can be mixed together and some will mix together well; some will dissolve; some will absorb liquids and others will not.
- Mixtures can sometimes be separated again into their components by sieving or filtering.
- Some substances change when they are heated and sometimes changes can be reversed and sometimes they cannot.
- The processes of melting, freezing, evaporation and condensation do not change what a substance is made from.

Physical processes: forces and motion

Children need to learn about how things respond to forces on the Earth. The child's world is full of instances of forces in action.

Check:
- Forces may be pushes or pulls which act on things in particular directions and can be measured.
- When objects are stretched or compressed, they also exert forces on whatever is stretching or compressing them.
- Forces may change the shape of something, make things move or change the way they move.
- When something is not moving the forces acting on it are balanced; unbalanced forces can make things speed up, slow down or change direction.
- Gravity is a force which pulls things towards the Earth and it is this which gives objects weight.
- Friction is a force which resists movement and it affects the size of the force needed to move things.

- Magnets attract and repel other magnets, depending upon which poles are brought together.
- Magnets exert noticeable forces on some other materials and can be used to make something move.
- Magnets align themselves roughly North–South when they are able to turn freely.

Physical processes: energy

Concepts related to the various aspects of *Energy* to be studied by children in the primary school mainly include aspects of light, sound, electricity and heat as they experience them directly in the world around them.

Check:
Electricity:
- Electricity only flows when there is a complete circuit of conducting material for it to flow around.
- Insulating materials resist the flow of electricity.
- The amount of electricity which can flow in a circuit (the current) depends upon the battery (the voltage) and the materials (the resistance) in the circuit.
- Bulbs, switches, buzzers and other components may be connected in a circuit in series or parallel.

Light:
- Some objects produce light and some reflect it; some objects obstruct light, causing shadows, and some let it pass through.
- Objects are seen because of the light which they either produce or reflect.
- Light normally travels in a straight path; mirrors can reflect light, changing its direction.
- Eyes are light detectors; we see because light from objects enters our eyes.

Sound:
- Sound spreads out from a source, travelling in all directions and gradually becoming fainter as it spreads; loud sounds can travel further than quiet sounds.
- Sound is produced by objects which are vibrating and objects of different sizes and shapes vibrate at different rates and give sounds of different pitches.
- Ears are sound detectors; we hear when sound vibrations enter our ears.
- Sound travels through solids, liquids and gases, but travels in some substances more easily than in others.

Heat:
- Heat energy is passed from hot substances to cold substances, making them warmer.
- Heat makes some substances change their state (from solid to liquid or liquid to gas); this can be useful.
- Some substances are better conductors of heat than others.
- Temperature is a measure of how hot or cold something is.

Physical processes: Earth and Beyond

Some aspects of *Earth and Beyond* can be quite difficult to teach because of their abstract and remote nature and many of the more interesting activities are best done at night.

Check:
- The Sun, the planet Earth and the Moon are approximately spherical.
- The Earth turns on its own axis, so we have day and night, with each complete turn taking 24 hours.
- The Earth is held by the gravity of the Sun; it orbits the Sun, taking one year to complete an orbit.
- Because the Earth's axis is tilted, some parts of the planet receive more heat and light from the Sun at certain times of the year, giving us the seasons.
- The Moon is a small planet-like body which orbits the Earth, taking one month for this cycle.
- The apparent shapes of the phases of the Moon are due to part of it being in shadow; we see it from different angles at different times.
- The Earth is only one of the planets of our Solar System.

To help the children understand these ideas, teachers will need to use a variety of strategies, as described in Chapter 5. They will also need to know and think about the ideas the children are bringing to the learning experiences to begin with.

Children's ideas in science

Primary children have a variety of incorrect, incomplete and fairly accurate ideas about living things, materials and their properties and physical processes which they bring to their science lessons. Often, these ideas will be based on limited experience, and may be partially or inaccurately constructed. Before introducing new ideas, teachers need to determine

- Prior to a staff meeting, ask teachers to note any of the children's ideas, unusual or otherwise, which the children in their class have put forward during science activities. Ask them to bring their list of ideas to the next staff meeting or staff development session on science.
- You could perhaps limit their list by asking them to focus on one idea from each of Sc2 (living things), Sc3 (materials) and Sc4 (physical processes).
- At the meeting, you should encourage teachers to discuss what they notice about the nature and quality of children's ideas at different ages and for the different areas of science.
- This could be carried out as a paper exercise and the responses collated for a more detailed discussion in which you could present some of the ideas from research about children's ideas in science.

what children already know and understand, and what experiences they bring with them to the classroom. This is an area where you, as the science coordinator, can provide them with some guidance.

Some particularly interesting aspects of primary children's ideas in science follow, to help you in your discussions with colleagues. In particular, you need to think about ways in which you can help colleagues to address starting points like these.

Some children's ideas about living things

There is an interesting account of the Zapotec civilization in Mexico in the 16th century, who believed that something was alive if it had 'breath' or 'wind'. For them, clouds, the white water of a river and the froth on a drink all had this vital force. Children, too, can have their own definitions of life. Young children may believe that only people, and possibly their pets, are alive. Research in Japan has shown that young children who raised goldfish at home had significantly more understanding about animals generally than those who had no pets or only had contact with animals at school (Hatano and Inagaki, 1992). Young children also tend not to see themselves as animals and so place people in a different category.

Research shows that children do not develop their ideas about life processes all at once. Qualter (1996) provides a useful account of the development of children's understanding of the processes of life. From having no concepts at all, young children (KS1) rapidly acquire ideas related to growth first and then movement. As children pass through primary school, these two life processes are consolidated at KS2 and supplemented by the beginnings of ideas related to respiration (or, more accurately, breathing) and simple reproduction. The remaining life processes are not acquired until the children are older. Since children develop ideas about to how things grow and move first, topics in science could focus upon these life processes by looking at how people, pets and other animals grow and move. Revisiting the experiences when the children are older allows a shift of focus to other life processes, like nutrition, respiration and reproduction. Again, children bring their own partly formed or wrong ideas about these processes. A developing chick inside a bird's egg might be thought by some children to be a collection of loose body parts floating about until they join together when the time is right (Harlen, 1992).

Some children may not see green plants as living things at all and fail to recognise life processes which parallel those in animals. For example, plants are not seen as being able to move. An animal's ability to move is more obvious. Plant movement is usually much more limited, and to children they often appear stationary. In a similar way, children may think that a plant takes in food through its roots, where the 'food' is of the same form as for animals. They may also believe that all wild animals are dangerous and attribute conscious choice to effects (for example, trees drop their leaves or animals change colour wilfully).

Some children's ideas about materials

One problem children have with materials is caused by the different uses of the term itself. The general use, as it relates to cloth and textiles, can cause the initial misconception that only fabrics are materials. Later, the idea of materials as the substance from which an item is made may cause confusion. Some children may be unable to distinguish between the functional parts and the materials of an object. When asked what a spoon is made from, they will say a handle and a scoop, rather than plastic and steel.

Some children may also have difficulty in linking cause and effect, particularly in slow changes. For instance, it can take some time before they are able to understand the changes in a compost heap or a decaying log as a continuous process. Terms like melting and dissolving may also be confused and used synonymously because they lack a model of what happens and what distinguishes the two.

Some children's ideas about physical processes

Since children's ideas about forces and motion include a belief that gravity pulls us down, they may resolve the problem of life on the other side of the world by depicting people as standing on their heads. Young children often believe things float because they are small, or conversely, they sink because they are big or because there is insufficient water. Another difficulty they have is in knowing what teachers mean by floating. They may consider an object to be floating only when all of it is above the surface of the water. This may be supplemented with an additional idea that some things are partly floating (or partly sinking). With magnetism, until they can distinguish different types of metals, they are likely to identify things made from any metal as being attracted to a magnet.

One of the misconceptions relating to energy that teachers will need to confront is that of energy as a physical entity. This gives rise to related misconceptions, like coal or gas are energy, or a battery is full of energy. Such misconceptions are reinforced by some advertisements for sweets or breakfast cereals.

Children's misconceptions about electricity include 'lumpy lectric' to explain what happens when they have a faulty connection. They may have the idea that if a socket is switched on with nothing plugged in, then the electricity will run out. Very young children can hold ideas that electricity, like water, is stored in walls. Turn on the tap or press the switch and out pours the water or electricity. Another misconception is that electricity flows from a battery to a bulb and makes it glow, so a return wire to complete the circuit is not necessary.

That light travels from the eye to the object is a common misconception held by some adults and children. Others think we look through a glow of light which serves to make things visible to us. Similarly, confusion over sources and reflectors of light exists, particularly with bodies like the Moon or a mirror. When beginning work on shadows, children may think that if an object like a ball is placed in the shadow of another object, like a wall, the place behind the ball will be twice as dark as the rest of the shadow.

Young children also have ideas about the Earth in space. They may believe that the Earth is flat, like a floating dinner plate, or else like a slightly flattened football which is occupied on only the upper surface. Once the idea of a spherical Earth develops, the misconceptions associated with the effects of gravity lead to incorrect ideas about how people on the opposite side of the world exist. Night and day as due to the Earth's rotation can also be a problem. It is easier to see the Sun moving across the sky than to represent a turning planet mentally. Finally, the scale of space can be difficult to internalise.

Strategies to support the construction of knowledge and understanding

One of your tasks as the science coordinator will be to encourage the teachers in your school to teach for understanding as well as acquiring new knowledge. There are a number of strategies teachers can use to teach, shape and elaborate knowledge and develop understanding, some of which were described in Chapter 5.

Think about:
- Orienting children towards the topic and eliciting prior relevant knowledge, looking for useful and inadequate conceptions.
- Asking children to clarify and explain their ideas.
- Encouraging discussion and debate of ideas.
- Providing experience of a new idea.
- Confronting misconceptions with contrary experience, where feasible.
- Confronting misconceptions with alternative scientific explanations.
- Explaining by bridging from the known to the unknown using specific examples, metaphors and analogies, and by modelling.
- Having the children predict and test their predictions.
- Having the children apply their knowledge and understanding in new situations.

Although this is a list, if you present it to your colleagues for discussion during a staff development session, as suggested on page 69, you will need to emphasise that it is not intended to imply a particular teaching order or that all strategies must always be used at any one time. Nor is it complete — your colleagues may well add others.

Suggestion

- If you can, observe some of your colleagues teaching science and note the questions they ask during the lesson.
- During a discussion, ask your colleagues to think about the questions they ask in science. When do they ask them? Why do they ask them? What purpose do they serve?
- If possible, compare what they think they do with what they really do. If you have been unable to carry out any observation, then refer back to the research evidence to stimulate the discussion.
- Do the children ask questions? How often? Why?

Questioning

A few well-planned questions will help children focus on a topic and help the teacher find out what they already know and understand. In teaching about friction, for instance, we might begin with: *'Did anyone slip on the ice this morning?'*, *'Why is ice slippy?'* and, *'Why are some things more slippery than others?'* Responses are not always accepted at face value. Further questions will require from the children clarification and explanation: *'So you think it is because ice is smooth. Why do you think being smooth makes a difference?'* Other children should be brought into the discussion: *'What do you think, John? Is your idea different?'* or *'Is that a good idea, Sarah? Why do you think so?'* Encourage your colleagues to think about the questions they ask in the classroom.

Hands-on experience

Providing experience of a phenomenon may involve hands-on exploration, directed activity, independent investigation and problem solving. It cannot always be a practical activity although we might like to aim for a high proportion to be so. For example, you could suggest that teachers could introduce the idea of energy as a state (something waiting to change) rather than an entity, using toys with visible springs. Stiff paper wound onto a pencil to make a spiral will turn as it is released, demonstrating the same phenomenon. The aim is to make the point visible and, wherever possible, tangible. Children may bring ideas which need to be changed. If they think that more wheels will make a buggy go faster, they can try it for themselves and see that the evidence is against them. Some beliefs, like thinking that plants do not move, can be confronted by contrary experiences. Certain plants, like the sensitive mimosa plant which can close its leaves when touched or an insectivorous plant (like the Venus fly trap or the sundew) show obvious movement.

Suggestion

Collect from your colleagues any ideas that they have come across to help make difficult or abstract ideas more concrete, perhaps using everyday objects like toys. Add these to your resource bank of ideas and, perhaps, build some expenditure into your budget for such items.

Alternative explanations and bridging analogies

Children commonly hold misconceptions about floating and sinking. A useful concept to help children to understand flotation is 'heavy for its size'. Things that are heavy for their size (we would say dense) tend to sink (denser than water). On this basis, big but hollow objects like ships are relatively light for their size, so tend to float. Had they been solid instead of hollow, they would be heavy for their size and so sink. Similarly, explaining energy in terms of something waiting to change is another example already described. Explanation of this kind would be used persistently in a variety of situations.

Ideas about evaporation can be supported by providing a bridge from the known to the unknown. You can suggest that your colleagues start with the things the children are familiar with, such as a plate of hot food. In a warm room, they cannot see the vapour rising from the food. However, if they take their plate of steaming food into a cold room, the water vapour can be seen to rise from the food. Then the children can be shown a hot, wet tea-towel. In the warm room they cannot see the water evaporating, but hang it outside in the cold air and the water vapour can be seen. The same wet tea-towel hung outside on a hot day would still have water evaporating from it but we would not be able to see it.

Using analogies can help teachers to bridge between the known and the unknown, but they can be quite difficult to think of. Some examples you might share with your colleagues include:

- Adaptation for life above and below the sea can be compared by paralleling the crab on the sea bed with a person on land and the fish with a bird.
- An analogy which may be used for gravity is that it is like walking on a surface covered with glue. When you lift your foot threads of glue pull it back. The higher you lift it, the more threads break until you are free of the glue — you escape gravity's pull. On the Moon the glue is not as sticky. On Jupiter, it is much stickier.
- For electricity, an analogy with water flowing through a tube commonly serves to bridge the children's ideas. The water represents the current flow and the tube the wire. A soap dispenser pump can be used to represent the battery. Another analogy used for electricity is that of circuit training. A line of children represents the current flow.

A piece of chocolate represents the push of the battery. Moving round the circuit, the children have to do things (jump over something, skip, lift a heavy bag from the floor to the table). When they return to the battery, they receive another square of chocolate. Increase the number of squares of chocolate and they have to move around the circuit faster.

- Analogies are also common for light and sound. Reflections of light are commonly described as being like balls bouncing from a wall or snooker balls being bounced from the side cushion of the table. The movement of sound through air is often compared to that of a compression wave travelling along the length of a slinky spring.

- With magnetism, the idea of an invisible hand with invisible fingers that can stretch out to push or pull can be a useful way to introduce magnetic forces. All analogies have their limits and, of course, with teachers you would need to emphasise that it is only *as though* there is an invisible hand there.

Models

With living things, using models to represent the organism can help. For example, a life-size skeleton can be constructed from cardboard tubes and boxes, connected with tape hinges and polystyrene balls on threads to represent joints. Rubber-band muscles complete the model. With older children, constructing robot-like figures from different shaped building blocks (like cuboids, cylinders, prisms of various shapes and sizes) can help to establish the idea of a variety of different cells making up an organism's body. In a similar way, a typical animal cell can be modelled using a small ball (the nucleus) in a stout transparent polythene bag (the cell membrane) filled with non-fungicidal wallpaper paste (the cytoplasm).

Modelling is one of the best ways to represent the Earth and beyond. The actual movements of the Earth and the other bodies, like the Moon, can be modelled readily. Using the children themselves to act out the motion can help to make it seem real. Similarly, a scale model, which starts with

Suggestion

Search professional journals for ideas for modelling concepts in science which may be difficult to explore in other ways. Add these to your resource file.

Venus represented by a pea and uses the school field to expand across the Solar System, can also help with an appreciation of scale, although a scale for the planets which can be handled by primary children means that the Sun cannot be true to the same scale. Actual observations of the night sky, records of the phases of the Moon, a trip to an observatory, or a visit to a planetarium are all ways to introduce ideas to do with Earth and Beyond.

Many of the concepts and generalisations we want the children to acquire may be used (and hence elaborated and consolidated) in new situations. For instance, when making powered buggies in Design and Technology, ideas about energy are applied to power the vehicles. As the coordinator for science, you must also be aware of the cross-curricular opportunities which are possible and which help children to apply their scientific skills, knowledge and understanding in new contexts. These are opportunities which may well be missed by colleagues and yet represent a way of working with which many of them are likely to feel comfortable.

A strategy for supporting teachers

When colleagues come to you for help with science, they often need support in bringing together the two aspects of science education: subject content knowledge (what to teach) and subject specific pedagogical knowledge (how to teach it). You may well find that it is the former that is worrying them, but in reality the science skills and concepts are relatively straightforward. The pedagogical knowledge is the bigger part and a non-specialist in science will quickly see its relevance. By emphasising this aspect, you will find your advisory role relatively easy because teachers will identify readily with what you are suggesting they do.

Since you may be asked for advice at a moment's notice, a supply of blank ideas sheets will be helpful to jot down thoughts during your discussion and also serve as a resource for the future. Figure 7.1 (p. 96) provides an example of the sort of sheet you might use.

FIG 7.1
Teaching ideas sheet

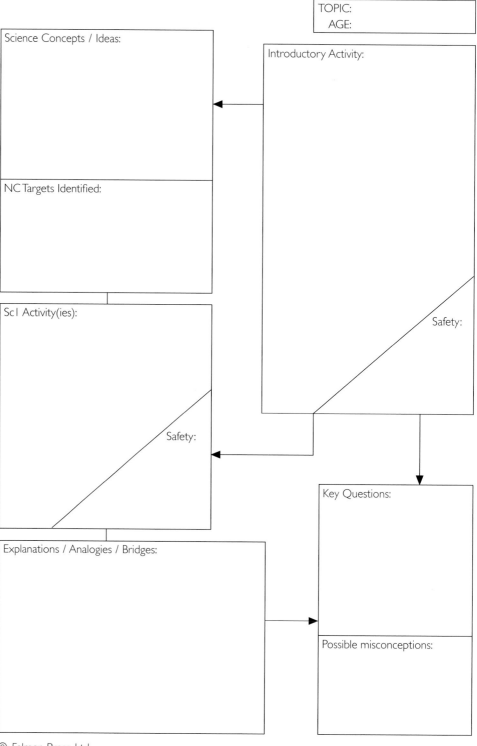

TOPIC:
   AGE:

Science Concepts / Ideas:

NC Targets Identified:

Introductory Activity:

Safety:

Sc1 Activity(ies):

Safety:

Explanations / Analogies / Bridges:

Key Questions:

Possible misconceptions:

© Falmer Press Ltd

Using a sheet like the one in Figure 7.1 also has the advantage of providing advice in a written form and your colleague can use it as a prompt for planning. At the same time, if you also make a copy for yourself, you will not only have a record of your discussion and the advice given, you will also soon build up a supply to draw on in the future.

To use such an ideas sheet, the science content is noted in the top left block, and the National Curriculum links are identified underneath. This will usually be very brief, perhaps one or two sentences only. Some teachers tend to bite off rather large chunks of science and this is a chance for you to break it down into more manageable units. It gives you an opportunity to target their teaching on the key skills and concepts.

The remaining blocks are for noting ideas on how to teach the selected topic. As the coordinator, you should be familiar with the teacher's preferred way of working and plan accordingly. Introductory ideas are those which help the children recall relevant prior knowledge and experience and also reveal any misconceptions. These may be some simple practical activities, in which case a note on safety may also be in order.

Key questions will be those which focus on the key concepts and also elicit relevant prior knowledge. Sometimes, children's prior knowledge and misconceptions about a topic are well known and so the teacher can be forewarned by you about what to anticipate.

Whenever feasible, suggest one or two science explorations or investigations, to be noted in the Sc1 Activity block. Ensure that these provide the opportunities for developing children's skills as described in Chapter 6. Again, anticipate matters of safety.

As in any subject, there are explanations and bridging strategies like analogies which are frequently used in connection with particular concepts and ideas. These are noted in the final block to help teachers support understanding and ensure some uniformity of practice across the school.

If your school staff plan ahead together, then these sheets (see Figure 7.1) could be used as a starting point for the planning meeting for science. Some time during a staff meeting could be used to explain the function of the sheet to all staff. Teachers can then work together to complete one for a topic with which they all feel comfortable (for example, topics like 'Seeds' or 'Ourselves'). This can be followed by one for a topic with which they are less familiar, chosen by you and where your input could be planned by you in advance.

The aim is to complete the sheet through discussion with the teacher, who should then feel that they have contributed as much as possible to the planning. You should avoid simply telling someone what to do, if at all possible. Try using, instead, phrases like, *'This worked well for me . . .'*, or *'With her class, Sue found . . .'* or *'I saw a good idea for that on TV you could try . . .'* These are useful 'think alouds' which will make your colleagues feel more comfortable about asking for advice. Interaction of this nature needs considerate handling since teachers are admitting to you their weaknesses and may feel very uncomfortable about doing so.

Summing up

In this chapter we have discussed some of the main points relating to the teaching of Sc2, Sc3 and Sc4 which may present problems for your colleagues and where your support as a coordinator may be needed. We have explored some strategies you may use in providing the necessary support, including a cooperative planning sheet. Some difficulties you might anticipate and plan for include:

■ your colleagues' own lack of knowledge and understanding in science;

■ their inability to bring together the science ideas and how to teach them in effective ways; and,

■ sensitive handling of advice when supporting colleagues in this way.

We have made some suggestions on how to approach these problems; more ideas relating to this aspect of your role will be found in subsequent chapters.

Chapter 8

Science and the whole curriculum

Introduction

The National Curriculum Council (NCC, 1990) suggested that some aspects of the curriculum were not sufficiently explicit in the National Curriculum Orders and yet permeate all the separate areas of experience. To this end, the NCC suggested a Whole Curriculum framework in which the National Curriculum could be embedded. The NCC identified three whole curriculum elements: cross-curricular dimensions, themes, and skills.

As the science coordinator, as well as monitoring the planning and delivery of science generally, one of the things you will need to check is that your school's science policy contains specific reference to these elements of the whole curriculum. You will also need to consider in some detail how these are provided. In particular, you should relate the dimensions, themes and skills to the criteria for good practice identified in the government's science policy statement (DES, 1985), described on page 21. In this chapter, we will discuss these elements, focusing, in particular, on those which are likely to fall within your brief as the science coordinator.

Dimensions

The cross-curricular dimensions are concerned with providing equal opportunities for all pupils so that they are prepared

With your colleagues, discuss some of the sources of negative attitudes towards science and origins of stereotypical images. Identify some possible ways forward to eradicate these conceptions. You could think about:

- the groups in which the children work: single sex or mixed; do they vary with task?
- the way teachers allocate tasks and activities to children: do the girls tend to be given so-called 'female' oriented tasks, like looking after the pets or plants; do the boys get most opportunity for working with construction kits?
- the textual resources used in the school (schemes, library books, wall charts): do they reinforce inappropriate attitudes?
- the language and gestures teachers themselves use: do they inadvertently present stereotypes (for example, the female primary teacher who tells the class she has done very little science and does not really like it).

Emphasise the need to begin early to your colleagues, starting with the children in the Reception class and building on it. Try expanding understanding by:

- drawing on examples from the history of science of female scientists and their work;
- invite scientists from a local university to come into school and give a talk about why they like science — undergraduate students may do this well;
- if possible, arrange a visit to where children can see both male and female scientists at work as a team.

Do not expect complete success overnight. The school is only one player in shaping children's conceptions.

broadly for adult life and a multicultural society. The science education being offered in your school should provide equal opportunities for all pupils, ensuring that they find tasks and activities relevant and interesting irrespective of their sex, ability, cultural or religious backgrounds.

In science, in particular, you will need to ensure that some children do not estrange themselves from the subject through prejudice or inappropriate conceptions of science and the scientist. For example, the popular view that girls can do the biological sciences and boys the physical sciences is unhelpful. Attitudes are formed at a very early age and are shaped by the home and the media, as well as experiences in school.

Newton and Newton (1997) found that:

- children as young as 6 years old have already developed a stereotypical image of scientists as male, white, bearded, slightly balding, with spectacles and a special coat;
- children place their scientists alone in laboratories with chemicals and glassware;
- the National Curriculum for Science has made little difference to this.

As the coordinator, you will need to check that such attitudes are not being inadvertently nurtured by the actions and attitudes of your colleagues or by the resources that they are using in school. You should ensure that teachers encourage and support positive attitudes towards science in both boys and girls. Interest alone is not sufficient to help a child overcome peer group prejudice and media images. Such influence may need to be addressed more directly. As a staff, you and your colleagues should discuss this matter and, as the coordinator, you should have some ideas about how you can deal with this potential problem.

Cultural diversity also needs to be reflected in the provision for equal opportunities in science. The science education offered should take account of the cultural diversity within the school, the community and society at large. What is meant by science may vary from culture to culture and children's prior experiences may be different in this respect. There may also be language difficulties for children for

Suggestion

- You should find out about the development of science in a variety of cultural contexts and also during different periods of history; these can be used as a source of ideas for your colleagues.
- Find out more about the beliefs of other cultures to see whether any ideas can be built into the science programme (for example, during work on food and nutrition, consider using examples of foods from various cultures; a talk with the RE coordinator or adviser could be helpful).
- If your school does not have a multicultural community to draw upon, perhaps you could make contact with a school in another town or city with which you, the staff and the children could work.

whom English is not the first language. Science has its own language, which may be complex. As coordinator, you are in a position to check that the books and resources used in science take into account cultural diversity and avoid propagating stereotypical images. This is something you can easily check when you buy new resources.

Themes

The cross-curricular themes identified by the NCC are concerned with the application of skills and knowledge to the real world, with self-development and values and beliefs. In particular, they are intended to develop the individual's sense of place within the community through the themes of Economic and Industrial Understanding; Education for Citizenship; Careers Education; Environmental Education; and Health Education. The last two in particular overlap work in science and you may find they are your responsibility.

Health education offers children opportunities to develop knowledge and understanding about exercise and health, diet and nutrition, personal hygiene, substance abuse, family life and sex education. These obviously overlap work on humans as organisms in Sc2: *Life Processes and Living Things*.

Environmental education is concerned with developing in children a knowledge and understanding of natural processes in the environment and how humans can influence these processes. This leads to studies of environmental issues like pollution, the greenhouse effect, acid rain and so on, all of which relate directly to the strand relating to living things in their environment (Sc2).

> *Think about:*
> - comparing the NCC (1995) guidance on the cross-curricular themes with the NC Order for Science at KS1 and KS2.
> - listing the ways in which the themes Health Education and Environmental Education can be achieved through your science education programme at KS1 and KS2.
> - identifying the resources available, both in school and outside, for delivering these.

Skills

The NCC (1990) identified six clusters of core skills which pervade the statutory National Curriculum: numeracy; problem-solving; study; social; communication; and information technology. The NCC considered that it is,

 ... absolutely essential that these skills are fostered across the whole curriculum in a measured and planned way. (1990, p. 3)

Communication and information technology (IT) skills are particularly relevant to science and your colleagues may need some guidance from you about how they can develop them to best effect. Your thinking can be informed by discussions with the English and IT coordinators in your school, so you should talk with them first. However, it will be your task to interpret Communication and IT in the context of science.

Communication skills and science

A requirement of the Programmes of Study for Science is that pupils should be taught to express themselves clearly in speech and in writing, to use scientific vocabulary appropriately and to use a variety of ways to present information. One of your tasks will be to check that teachers are providing opportunities for this and you may need to give some guidance.

Communication is both a physical and a mental activity. It is valuable in the context of science because both children and teachers can learn something from the activity. The children, through communication with others in various ways, learn to:
- make sense of experiences, clarify ideas and knit them together;
- sort ideas into a logical order, sequence events and decide what is important and what can be omitted;
- produce a structure or framework to represent the overall experience and synthesise the ideas;
- develop and use scientific vocabulary in different contexts and apply various language skills;

At a staff meeting, ask colleagues to think about the different ways they usually encourage their children to communicate in science lessons. Some particular aspects you could explore include:

- Why should children communicate in science?
- What forms of communication do colleagues most often use?
- Which forms seem to be most frequently used with children of different ages?
- Which forms seem to be most frequently used for different topics in science?
- What purposes do different forms of communication serve?

■ step back and examine experiences from different perspectives and reflect on them.

Your colleagues should view communication activities as part of the overall learning experience and not simply as evidence that opportunities for learning were provided.

Since children are to communicate in various ways during science activities, the forms of communication used should be appropriate for the science activity and relevant to the needs and abilities of the children. You will need to ensure that your colleagues are aware of the variety of forms available and how they can be used for different purposes in science. These can be loosely grouped as:

- *Oral communication*: e.g. discussion between pupils, between a pupil and teacher, tape-recorded accounts, oral presentations to others (group, class, school).
- *Written communication*: e.g. free writing, structured worksheets, sequential accounts of experiments and investigations.
- *Graphic communication*: e.g. pictures, before-and-after drawings, cartoon strip sequences, labelled diagrams, graphs, charts and tables.
- *Other forms of communication*: e.g. photography, audio and video recordings, dramatic productions, model making, information technology.

The final question your colleagues may ask about children communicating in science concerns the type of recording that is suitable for children of different ages and abilities. The answer is that there is no hard and fast rule. Each should be considered relative to the task. The degree of teacher support will also determine which is appropriate. The aim is to give children experience of a variety of methods so that, eventually, they are able to select for themselves the most appropriate one to use. Of course, children do not need to record and communicate everything they do in science and you will need to make this clear to your colleagues.

Information technology skills and science

Information is a valuable acquisition and, throughout our lives, we use our brains to process and store it. Purposeful activity is impossible without it. Writing and reading skills have reduced the burden of information storage. Similarly, the development of tools such as the electronic calculator and the desktop computer have aided the processing of information. Information technology (IT) in its broadest sense can be used in science, not only for word- and number-crunching using computers, but also in devices like tape and video recorders, fax machines, photocopiers and cameras. Although the use of IT in primary schools has been steadily growing, its use to support children's learning in science is less well developed.

Talking with your colleagues, you will discover that it is easy to find reasons for this — a shortage of worthwhile hardware and software and some teachers' lack of experience could be high on their list. However, the requirement in science is that:

> Pupils should be given opportunities, where appropriate, to develop and apply their information technology (IT) capability in their study of science. (DfE, 1995, p. 1)

In the programme of study for Key Stages 1 and 2 which has become known as Sc0 (the requirements to be applied across Sc1, Sc2, Sc3, and Sc4) it states as an aspect of systematic enquiry that:

> Pupils should be given opportunities to . . . (d) use IT to collect, store, retrieve and present scientific information.
>
> (DfE, 1995, pp. 2, 7)

Many schools have appointed a coordinator for IT. If there is such a person in your school then it makes sense for you to work with him or her to plan and implement a programme which incorporates IT in science.

IT should be accepted as a legitimate part of science, as a tool used to facilitate thinking and working. IT skills are useful for acquiring scientific knowledge and understanding, both in and out of school. It has the potential to extend someone's competence in many facets of life — in the home, at work and in leisure. Since these are often science and technology related, the information processing and handling skills developed and practised at school have a wider application. In developing IT skills, children are encouraged to develop logical thinking, problem-solving abilities and information-finding capabilities, all valuable in science.

Finally, there is a need to develop a critical awareness of the role of information technology in science. It is important to know its strengths and weaknesses, not only what it can and cannot do, but also what it should and should not do. Information technology is a tool to achieve ends, not an end in itself.

Think about the potential uses of IT in science:
- Word Processing and General Communication Skills
- Accessing Information on CD-ROMs
- Data Handling and Presentation: Spreadsheets and Data Bases
- Sensing the Environment
- Modelling, Games and Simulations
- Using the Information Superhighway

As the coordinator, choosing software for use in science will probably also be one of your responsibilities. This is, in some ways, no different to choosing a good textbook to use with the class.

Think about what you want the software to do:
- to communicate successfully;
- to use effective teaching strategies;
- be an interesting and worthwhile alternative to other ways of working.

At the same time, there are important differences between a piece of software and a textbook. For example, a book is deaf to the response of the reader, while the computer can enter into some form of dialogue, depending upon the software. However, a book needs no introduction or instruction manual on how to use it, it can be borrowed easily and it does not need a power supply. It also tends to be much more portable and tolerant of abuse than the computer. The physical differences between textbooks and computers tend to conceal a common purpose, that is to support effective teaching and learning. Nevertheless, it is useful if you can

FIG 8.1
A software evaluation schedule

A SOFTWARE EVALUATION SCHEDULE

Software Title: .... *System:* .... *Cost:* ....

Some general considerations:

1 Is the cost acceptable?

2 Are the teacher's notes adequate?

3 Can the package be used with little or no teacher support?

   i is the verbal information too difficult?

   ii are the illustrations or graphics likely to be effective?

   iii can a wrong key be pressed without things going wrong?

4 Can effects that may disturb others (e.g. sound) be switched off?

If the answer to some or all of these is no, is it worth proceeding?

Some considerations regarding its role as a teacher:

1 Does the instruction fit in with your scheme of work?

2 As far as you can judge, is the information correct and free from bias?

3 Does it provide the kind of learning you require (memorisation, understanding, application, problem solving...)?

4 Is it likely to achieve what you want as efficiently as other means?

5 Will those who use it find it interesting?

6 Does it provide opportunities for worthwhile participation?

7 Is feedback provided for the user?

8 Could it be used by children with a relatively wide range of ability?

9 Does it keep records of pupils' work?

Some considerations regarding its role as information handler (e.g. spreadsheet or database):

1 Does it do something that is relevant?

2 Does it process data and information in more than a trivial way?

3 If incorrect information is fed in, does it allow corrections without the teacher's help?

4 Does the package allow copies of pupils' work to be made?

Some considerations regarding its role in control:

1 Is the kind of control suited to the ability of the child?

2 Do the commands have meaning for the child?

3 Can unexpected commands be used without damage or injury?

Some considerations regarding its role as information presenter (e.g. word processor):

1 Are the pupils likely to cope with the commands, menus, etc?

2 Will the pupil be able to print unaided?

3 Is what you see on the screen what you get when it is printed?

4 Does it allow easy editing of the information at a later date?

Some considerations regarding its role as a source of information (e.g. library resource):

1 Are the pupils likely to cope with the commands, menus, key words, etc?

2 Will the pupil be able to print information unaided?

forget some of the physical differences between the two, and focus on judging the software as you would a textbook. You should think about the level at which the language is pitched, the choice of vocabulary, length of sentences, even the font used. What about the effectiveness of the illustrations — are real photographs preferable to cartoon characters? Do the characters move? There is also a need to consider the kind of learning which is supported: is it the recall of facts, procedures, understanding or application in new situations?

Differences between books and computers, however, cannot be ignored altogether. If a book is opened at the wrong page the mistake is easy to remedy. What happens if a wrong key is pressed? Does the system crash or does the child have to sit through screen after screen of information before getting back to where he or she wants to be?

To make the process of evaluating software more efficient, it is useful to use an evaluation schedule. The one provided in Figure 8.1 can be used to audit the software you already have for science or any you might be thinking of buying, enabling you to identify areas of strength and weakness. Resource needs and supplementary support for staff in the use of IT in science can be identified.

The first step is to determine the function of a piece of software. If this does not match the needs then it is pointless to proceed further. There are also some general criteria which should usually be met by the software, and some specific questions relating to how well the software fulfils its function. The answer of 'Yes' to most of the relevant questions usually indicates that the software package is worth trying with the children. Few things are perfect, however, so some 'No' responses may mean that the package is usable but needs some support. Remember that your colleagues must have an opportunity to try out a new piece of software before they use it with children.

Summing up

In this chapter we have considered the place of science within the whole curriculum and, in particular some dimensions, themes and skills which may have to be more specifically addressed through science. The responsibility for ensuring this may well be yours, as the science coordinator. Some difficulties you might anticipate and plan for include:

■ ensuring that children are genuinely provided with equal opportunities during their science education;
■ raising awareness of the variety of ways in which children can communicate in science for different purposes;
■ providing specific support on the use of IT in science.

Some ways forward have been suggested. In the next chapters we turn our attention to developing the science policy for your school and aspects of implementation.

Part three

Whole school policies and schemes of work

Chapter 9

Developing the school policy for science

Introduction

It is usually one of the major tasks of any coordinator to provide a framework for structuring the school policy for the area of the curriculum for which the coordinator is responsible. This policy has to be translated into action and then subjected to regular review. Edmonds and Manford (1996) provide a very useful list of points to guide you, as the coordinator, in developing your school's policy for science.

- Teaching staff need to recognise that there is a need for a policy.
- It must be clear who the policy is for.
- The outcomes of the policy must be specified.
- The time-scale for actions must be clear.
- Time must be given to gathering information at the outset.
- The initial policy should be produced in draft form.
- There must be time for staff to digest and discuss its implications.
- The redraft should take into account teachers' views and suggestions.
- The implementation should be monitored, evaluated and reviewed.

Once in place, Harrison (1995) suggests that a policy serves a number of useful purposes. It makes public the school's intentions for science, providing information for parents,

FIG 9.1
Plan for developing and
implementing a school
science policy

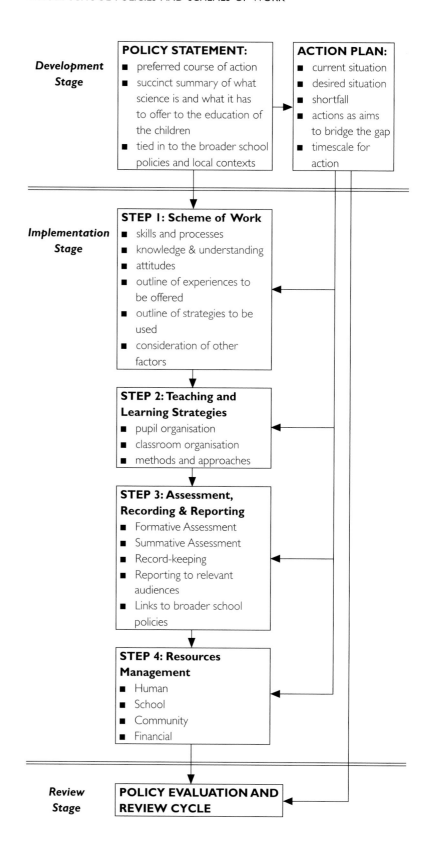

governors and others. It supports teachers, particularly those new to the school or less experienced, by letting them know what is valued and it can aid continuity and progression. It also highlights priorities, shapes future actions and helps to make a case for resources and funding.

The remainder of this chapter will describe the components of a policy statement for science and a system for developing and implementing it. These are summarised in Figure 9.1. This example offers you a framework which you could adapt to suit your particular situation.

The development stage: STEP I — *the science policy statement*

The first stage is to produce a general statement of intent regarding science in your school. This is the *Science Policy Statement* and it should be in a form that is suitable for teachers, governors, parents, LEA officials and OFSTED inspectors. It is likely to have more value and effect if all teaching staff have been involved in its development, and so you should circulate drafts for comments as it develops.

A *policy* is a course of action that is preferred above others and is to be actively supported. A policy statement makes this public in a statement of intent or an account of that preferred course of action. As such, the policy statement should usually be:
- written;
- general;
- succinct;
- in accord with the requirements of the Education Reform Act;
- intended to further a broader school policy; and,
- takes into account particular school and local situation.

It is not always easy to write a policy statement and as a consequence statements are produced which may be weak because:
- they do not identify favoured courses of action;
- they are too specific;

Suggestion

It is sometimes useful for a coordinator to ask colleagues the following questions:
- *What do you envisage science to be?*
- *What has it to offer children's education in our school?*
- *What are the particular and unique needs of the children in our school?*

Your colleagues need to share a common understanding of what science is and what science education is all about. This is your starting point for writing the policy statement.

- they do not adequately take into account the National Curriculum Order for Science;
- they are not in accord with a broader school policy; and/or,
- they ignore the unique educational aspects of the situation.

Weak policy statements often include unnecessary detail such as schemes of work and class timetables, both of which follow from an implementation of the policy, but should not be a part of the policy statement.

To write a science policy, you should begin with what the subject has to offer.

Next, state that there is a legal requirement to teach it. Tie it in to the broader general policies of the school, for example, those on assessment and teaching approaches. The policy statement should conclude with broad, general aims for science education in your school. These broad aims should be achievable, based on feasible practice and have clear targets. These will figure in the *action plan* you will then produce (see below).

It is advisable that the policy statement is drafted by you as the coordinator, perhaps in consultation with the headteacher and coordinators of other relevant areas (such as assessment). You can then circulate the draft to colleagues and governors for comments and discussion before you take any further action. Everyone involved in implementing the policy should have a chance to comment upon it. An example of one possible policy statement follows in Figure 9.2 (p. 115).

Development stage: STEP 2 — *the science action plan*

Your next step as coordinator is to draw up a *Science Action Plan*. An action plan states what actions are intended for achieving the policy. You may wish to append this to the policy statement (for example, as *Appendix: Plan of Action for Science*) or it could follow as the next section in the policy document. To prepare an action plan, you will need to be familiar with:

FIG 9.2
An example of a science policy statement

> ### Science: A Policy Statement
>
> Science figures in most aspects of modern life in our society. An understanding of its nature and some scientific knowledge is of value to our pupils as we prepare them for adulthood. Science offers the opportunity to acquire a way of thinking and working which can serve as a basis for understanding the world in which we live, it can be a model for solving problems and can satisfy personal needs like curiosity. Science can draw upon and illuminate a wide range of contexts. Science is also a required core subject in the National Curriculum for England and Wales.
>
> It is our policy as a staff to satisfy the requirements of the National Curriculum Order for Science and to develop scientific knowledge, understanding and skills in the pupils we teach. In accordance with the school policy regarding teaching approaches, we favour approaches which will make science relevant and meaningful to the children, drawing particularly on real world examples. In accordance with the school policy on equal access for all pupils to all curricular experiences, science will be taught in ways which make it accessible to all, regardless of gender, culture, race or ability. Assessment of science and the monitoring of progress will be in accordance with the National Curriculum Order and school policy, which favours formative assessment. Advantage will be taken of the many opportunities provided by scientific activities to develop collaborative skills, as well as individual skills such as communication and the use of information technology.

- the current situation regarding science teaching in the school;
- the desired situation, taking into account legal as well as personal and local requirements;
- the shortfall — prioritised statement of needs and actions to achieve the desired state; and,
- a programme of action.

The current situation

You will need to provide an objective statement of current practice in science throughout the school. It should be carefully and considerately worded so as not to alienate those teachers who may not yet be working in line with intended practice, and particularly those who may have to change their approaches and behaviours considerably. Information needs to be collected, to find out what is done in each class in the school.

Suggestion

A discussion with each class teacher is usually the best way to collect such information. A discreet look at children's work in books and displays can help to supplement it. If time is a problem, then you could circulate a simple list of questions to teachers, asking about what they did with their classes the previous year and what they are currently doing.

In the first instance, you will be checking that what is being provided is, at the least, likely to satisfy the National Curriculum requirements and consolidate, supplement or extend them. You should look for evidence of:

- providing appropriate contexts;
- developing broad and balanced knowledge and understanding;
- practising and developing a full range of investigation skills;
- progression within a year group and across years;
- continuity across key stages;
- appropriate tasks for assessment purposes;
- sound portfolios of assessment evidence; and,
- appropriate record-keeping.

The information you collect should show where there are gaps and weaknesses and where the school's policy is unlikely to be achieved. It will also highlight strengths which can be built upon. The results can be presented succinctly as a list.

The desired situation

This can be presented as a statement of specific goals or targets which follow from the policy statement and reflect the statement of intent. The Programmes of Study can provide these. You should also try to build upon the strengths which have been seen in the current situation and consider particular needs of the children.

The shortfall — prioritised needs

This states the gap between the desired situation and the current situation and also provides you, as coordinator, with a picture of where your main focus is going to be in the short-, medium-, and long-term for supporting colleagues. You need to be specific about what is needed to close the gap. Focus particularly on:

- shortfalls in knowledge and understanding
  (*e.g. omissions or unnecessary duplication*)
- shortfalls in practical experiences
  (*e.g. too much emphasis on observation and prediction; not enough full investigations with control of variables*)

FIG 9.3
An example of a programme
of action

Programme of Action for the Forthcoming Year

By the end of the Autumn Term we will have:
1 Examined a range of commercial schemes and chosen one.
2 Held an Autumn Fair to raise funds to buy the selected scheme.
3 Had a staff development session on 'Forces'.

By the end of the Summer Term we will have:
1 Established a progressive science programme.
2 Bought the selected scheme and integrated it into the programme.
3 Held a staff development day on investigative work in science and the use of IT.

- problems with resources
  (*e.g. lack of particular kinds of resources; organisation; access; safety; ...*)
- lack of progression and continuity.

For each target, you should try to suggest a possible solution.

The programme of action

You will next need to sort the shortfalls or targets into an order priority. It is useful to do this in consultation with your headteacher, as you will need to identify funding and resource needs, where appropriate. A discussion with the headteacher will also help you to draw up a time-scale of what might feasibly be achieved and when. It may be necessary to consider alternative sources of funding. You can then prepare a list of detailed actions with appropriate dates. Figure 9.3 above shows an example of such a programme.

At the end of the period covered by the action plan, you should review it with your colleagues, identify what progress has been made, discuss the next stage, and draw up the next action plan. Usually such plans develop into finer detail as time passes.

Implementation stage: STEP 1 — *a school science scheme of work*

Having developed the policy statement and action plan, your next step is to translate that statement of intent into a working document which can be put into practice at the classroom level. A starting point for this is often to consider a *scheme of work* for science which encapsulates the intentions of the policy statement.

A *scheme of work* is a written statement describing succinctly the experiences planned for all pupils over a specific period. This is usually for the full school year, as this has the advantage of allowing you, as coordinator, to check that broad and balanced science is being offered throughout the school and that it is continuous and progressive. As such, it becomes a statement of action, which:

- fits in with the overarching school policies;
- reflects a broad and balanced coverage of scientific skills and processes, knowledge and understanding, and desirable attitudes towards science;
- identifies in outline the means by which the experiences are being offered; and,
- suggests teaching and learning strategies and approaches to be used.

The scheme of work must also take into consideration:

- whole school plans;
- Year group or Key Stage plans;
- individual class teachers' preferences (particularly strengths);
- ease of use for new and inexperienced staff; and,
- availability to significant others (such as parents and governors).

Your school's scheme of work may be based upon a commercial scheme or it may be an agreed programme designed by you in cooperation with all the staff who must implement it.

There are two main ways in which you can begin to develop the science scheme of work, shown diagrammatically in Figure 9.4 (p. 119). The first method begins with the National Curriculum document itself. By looking at the Programmes of Study, group the elements to form complete activity clusters or topics. These can then be sorted into a year-by-year timetable which ensures all elements are included and breadth and balance are achieved. This suits

FIG 9.4
The two main approaches to planning the school science programme

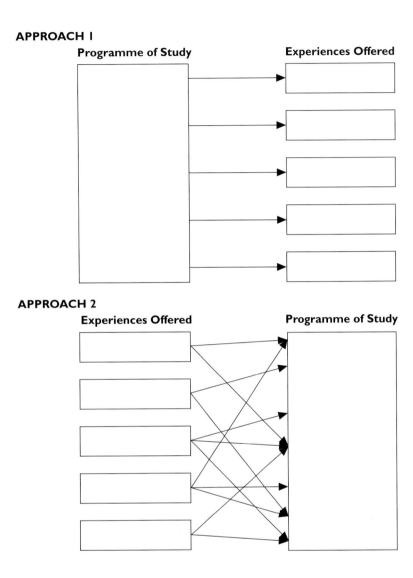

APPROACH I

Programme of Study   Experiences Offered

APPROACH 2

Experiences Offered   Programme of Study

approaches where science stands alone in the curriculum. However, you would be wise to involve colleagues in the allocation of the topics, giving them some choice according to their strengths and interests, if at all possible. As the science coordinator, you would in these circumstances also need to ensure that relevant contexts and opportunities for integration follow from this process.

Alternatively, it is possible to start with what your colleagues do now. Ask them to identify the range of themes or topics they would like to cover and then analyse the Programmes of Study to identify what has been covered. This suits situations

FIG 9.5

Topic list for planning the whole school programme

Tick (√) the topics you usually do with your class. Star (✗) those you might like to do.

Topic	N	R	Y1	Y2	Y3	Y4	Y5	Y6
Air								
Animals								
Autumn								
Birds								
Bridges								
Buildings								
Changes								
Christmas								
Clothes								
Colour and Light								
Communications								
Cookery								
Day and Night								
Eggs								
Electricity in Our Homes								
Energy								
Families								
Festivals								
Flight								
Floating and Sinking								
Flowering Plants								
Food								
Forces								
Gravity and Falling								
Growing Things								
Harvest Festival								
Health and Hygiene								
Hot and Cold								
Houses and Homes								
Keeping Warm								
Local Studies:								
farm								
field								
hedgerow								
park								
pond								
river / stream								
seashore								
street								
town								
wood								
village								
Magnets								
Materials								
Me/Myself								
Minibeasts								
Mirrors and Reflections								
Moving Around								
Ourselves								
Patterns								
People Who Help Us								
Pets								
Plants								
Plastics								
Pollution								
Pushes and Pulls								
Rocks and Fossils								
Seasonal Change								
Sky and Space								
Soils								
Sound and Music								
Spring								
Summer								
Sun and Shadows								
Symmetry								
Time								
Toys								
Transport								
Trees								
Water								
Weather								
Wet and Dry								
Wheels								
Windy Days								
Winter								
Add any missing topics								

© Falmer Press Ltd

where an integrated approach is used and the staff tend to feel more involved in its development and consequently happier with the outcome. The problem is that the coordinator must ensure that there is cohesion, that a broad and balanced set of experiences is being offered and that key areas of experiences are not being overlooked or omitted.

You should begin by taking teachers' strengths into account. Allocate as many of their chosen topics or preferences as possible to half-termly slots, bearing in mind the need for breadth and balance. The remainder of the programme can be filled by allocating topics that are not currently being covered but should be. This is best done by you through negotiation and gentle persuasion with your individual colleagues, and offering your help where needed. You could, perhaps, simultaneously identify what further in-service support you may need to provide to ensure the teachers feel confident and competent to deliver these new areas of experience. By allocating the same topic to different teachers at different times of the year it is also possible to reduce resource demands as well. Where a school has mixed age groups in one class, it is also allows you to plan for multiple year cycles. This will enable you to ensure that the children experience a progressive programme of experiences even though remaining with the same teacher for a second year. An example of how this was done in a six-class primary school is given in Figure 9.6 (p. 122).

In reality, a combination of the two methods are likely to suit most schools, since most Key Stage 1 teachers seem to operate in a cross-curricular way, while teachers of older Key Stage 2 pupils may be more subject focused, with a transition phase between the two. This is shown diagrammatically in Figure 9.7 (p. 123).

FIG 9.6
Example of a whole school programme for science

Class/ Teacher		AUTUMN TERM		SPRING TERM		SUMMER TERM	
		1st Half	2nd Half	1st half	2nd Half	1st Half	2nd Half
Pre-KS1	**Nursery**	Senses	People Who Help Us	Colour	Weather	Food	Seashore
	Reception	Harvest / Fruit & Veg.	Time / Day and Night	Weather	Water	Growing Things	■ Ourselves as Animals
KS1	**Year 1**	Day, Night & Seasons	Birds as Animals	Transport & Movement	Sound and Communication	Water — Floating & Sinking	Seashore
	Year 2	Me, Myself & My Family	Light and Colour	Water and Dissolving	■ Electricity	■ Magnetism	Seasons & Growth
Lower KS2	**Year 3**	Houses & Homes	Ourselves — Body and Health	Senses	■ Air	Plants and Soil	Seasonal Changes
	Year 4	Colour & Camouflage	Hot and Cold	Ourselves and Other Animals	Homes	■ Cookery & Changes	■ Sound and Music
Upper KS2	**Year 5**	■ Rocks and Fossils	■ Changes of State (SLG)	■ Magnetism	■ Forces and Their Effects	■ Exploring Environments: The Local Wood	■
	Year 6	Air and Flight	Earth in Space	Transport & Communication	Electricity in Our Homes	Colour & Light	Water & Flotation

Two teachers have mixed age classes (Y4/5 and Y5/6) to work a three-year rolling programme between them.

■ Additional topics to give breadth and balance and to ensure NC requirements are met. As far as is feasible, teachers still have at least four of the topics they like to teach.

FIG 9.7
Some common approaches for
organising primary science

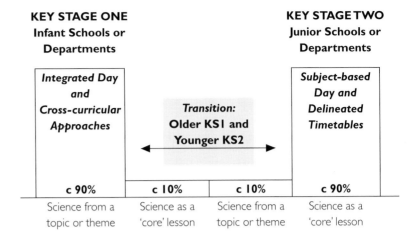

Implementation stage: STEP 2 — teaching and learning strategies

For the set of experiences you have outlined in the scheme to be successful, they must meet the needs of all the pupils in the class. As such, it is necessary for a coordinator to think about the various organisational and other strategies used in the school. This will require you to consider:

■ *pupil organisation* (whole school; whole class; group; individuals; equal opportunities);

■ *classroom organisation* (of the learning environment; of resources; of support mechanisms);

■ *teaching methods and approaches used* (starting from a knowledge/content base; starting from a skills/procedures base; problem-solving approaches; interaction strategies); and,

■ *safety* (the policy statement must provide for the implementation of a code of safe working practice which applies to all personnel, not only teachers, but teaching assistants, students, parents and others working in the school; there is likely to be a school safety policy in place which should be referred to).

These matters will be discussed in detail in Chapter 14.

Implementation stage: STEP 3 — *assessment, recording and reporting*

In general, the policy for science should relate to the whole school policy for assessment, recording and reporting of pupils' progress and achievements. As described in Chapter 13, there are different ways to assess, record and report for different purposes. When developing the policy statement and describing its implementation, you will need to show how and when assessments will be carried out and how evidence will be used to show progress. It will also be necessary for you to indicate recording and reporting mechanisms.

Implementation stage: STEP 4 — *resources management*

When discussing the management of resources it is easy to focus exclusively on science equipment and textual resources. While these are important, they represent only part of the resources in your school that you will be managing as the science coordinator. You will need to consider the range of other resources available:

- Human: teachers, pupils, parents and relatives, people and facilities in the community;
- School: rooms; wet and dry areas; open work areas; library; display opportunities (3-D as well as 2-D); storage areas and facilities; hardware and software for IT; television/video/audio facilities;
- Community: the local environment — streets; parks; playground areas; fields; woods; garden centres;
- Financial: budget details; allowances for science; consumable costs; one-off expensive items; safety and repair costs; funds for visits; sources of alternative funding.

You should draw up a comprehensive list of all resources (equipment, books, schemes, posters, IT, television, video, radio, other) which should be available to staff. A system for storage, use and return of resources should be designed,

Suggestion

Some sources of information you may find useful include:
- collect information about teachers' and children's perceptions of school science;
- collate standardised test results, SAT scores and summarise these graphically to show patterns;
- compare your school's results with local and national trends to give an overall feel for how things are going.

Some classroom observation (with the willing cooperation of the teachers concerned) might also generate ideas for in-service sessions and discussions on strategies and approaches.

which includes safety, repair and replacement considerations, as described in Chapter 14.

Review stage: STEP 1 — *policy evaluation and review*

You should plan for the science policy statement and its implementation to be reviewed regularly. The policy statement itself should be sufficiently general to survive minor alterations to the National Curriculum Order for Science, or staff changes in the school. However, you should carry out an annual review in which minor adjustments can be made and new actions planned. Occasionally, more substantial changes may be required to take into account new legislation or major staffing changes. This review process is one which again should involve all staff, since the consequences may affect classroom practice at various levels, although it may be relatively easy to circulate draft changes for comments.

To make it a more structured procedure, some measurement of the success or otherwise of the policy implementation might be included.

Summing up

In this chapter we have provided some details of how you can approach writing the school's policy statement and action plan for science. Some difficulties you might anticipate and plan for include:
- finding time to draft, circulate and finalise documents;
- collecting appropriate information which can be used for this purpose.

In the next chapter, we will consider how the school science policy is implemented.

Chapter 10

Policy into practice

Introduction

The key to good teaching and learning in any area of the curriculum is detailed and structured planning. As the curriculum leader, you may have to help a teacher to plan effectively in science and one way to do this is for you to provide a system based on familiar, tried and trusted approaches.

Areas like mathematics education, with a long history of being taught in primary schools, have well-developed bodies of practice and examples. This can indicate which activities are likely to be feasible and appropriate for a given group of children. Science teaching in the primary school, however, is still developing its body of practice. This relates to science as a body of knowledge and as a way of thinking and working, both set in relevant contexts. These various facets must be balanced in any science programme, a task which will inevitably fall first on you.

The National Curriculum for Science leaves a lot to be determined by individual teachers, particularly at the level of lesson planning and delivery. While this lack of prescription is to be welcomed, since it gives teachers freedom to select approaches and activities to suit the needs and interests of the children, it also means more work for you in terms of guidance, monitoring and evaluation. The remainder of this section provides you with some guidance to help you bridge the gap with colleagues between the National Curriculum Order, the school policy for science and classroom practice.

Contexts and strategies

There is a danger that activities in science will be perceived by children as being detached from what matters in the real world. At best, such activities might be seen as interesting pastimes; at worst, they are mere tasks to complete before home-time. Skills, knowledge and understanding, as specified in the National Curriculum Order, need to be embedded in relevant contexts. A good context can give an activity purpose and meaning and make learning last, so you will need to encourage teachers to set science experiences in contexts that allow pupils to appreciate the significance of their work and its relevance to everyday life.

Often, these contexts can arise from the broad topic or theme your colleagues are covering so that a number of curricular experiences are linked or integrated and are mutually supporting. In this way, you can support your colleagues with their planning by starting from points with which they are comfortable. For example, a topic like 'Houses and Homes' at either Key Stage 1 or Key Stage 2 could lead to exploring, investigating and experimenting with different materials, structures and forces and energy use, as well as allowing scope for design and technology (designing and making a house for the three pigs which is wolf resistant), history (house styles through time), geography (neighbourhood survey of types of houses), art (collage houses made from rubbings of building materials), mathematics (calculating surface area for buying new carpets or curtains), and language work (descriptive accounts about, for example, the chaos of moving home). This is a very familiar way of working for most teachers and one with which your colleagues are likely to feel confident. It is also easy for you to indicate the relevance of science in such contexts.

Each context needs an agenda and script; that is, what will be said and done to draw the children into the context, prepare and motivate them and then release them into the activity. This can be achieved in a number of ways. For example, stories and rhymes can provide the vehicle for young children. Sometimes serendipity — a fortuitous or spontaneous event — can serve as a starting point, particularly for problem-solving challenges with older pupils. Without your support and guidance, some teachers may miss such relevant opportunities, so you could design a planning guide for your colleagues. Figure 10.1 shows an example of a guide, indicating some of the things teachers might think about when setting science topics in context (see p. 129).

A system for structuring science experiences

A system you might use with teachers to develop their planning into structured delivery is shown in Figure 10.2 (p. 130). The context for activities is identified first. Any broad topics or themes being used to integrate the work are indicated, although it may be that some topics are too limited in scope and so a more science-focused topic may be needed. How it is to be presented in the classroom has to be agreed and an appropriate strategy selected.

Although the system is sequential, it is not always necessary to work through every step. For example, research indicates that when children have some relevant prior knowledge and experience, they may begin Step 3 at point 3.2 (Cavalcante, Newton and Newton, 1996).

Some illustrative examples of the procedure

It is sometimes useful to give your colleagues some examples of how planning can be structured using this procedure. This can help to focus their mind on what is needed. What follows are examples for the different phases and across Scl, Sc2, Sc3 and Sc4.

FIG 10.1
A guide for planning science topic work

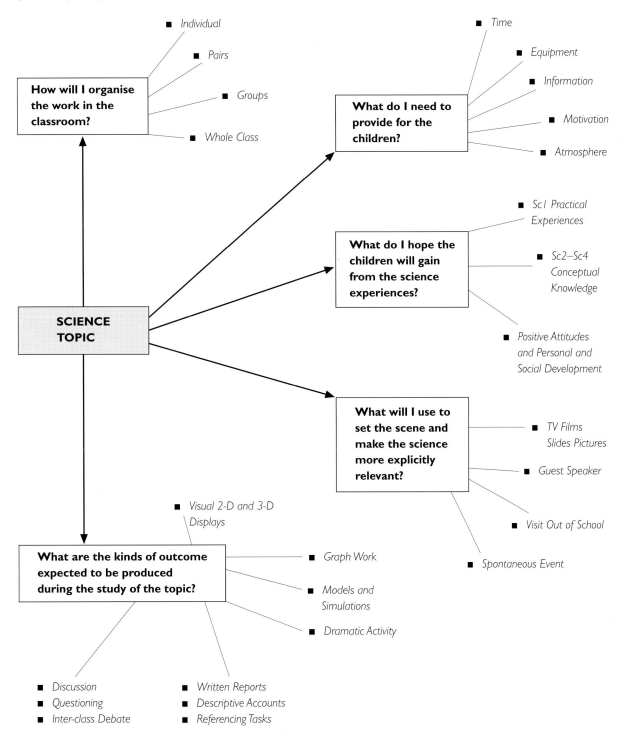

FIG 10.2
A guide for structuring science activity

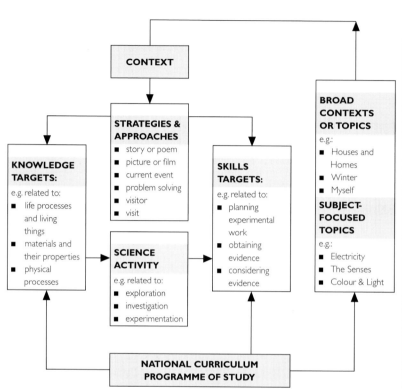

Using the system:
The system is quite simple and follows a sequence of steps, which you could work through with a teacher who needs support.

Step 1:
1.1 Consult the class records to determine what experiences the children have already had.
1.2 Look at the Programmes of Study for the relevant key stage.
1.3 Identify 'X' as something to be taught.

Step 2:
2.1 Consult your list of topics or themes for the term or year and identify one which provides a fairly ready and comfortable context for 'X'. For a fully integrated approach, select an introductory strategy.
or:
2.2 Consult your list of specific, focused or narrower topics and identify one which provides a fairly ready context for 'X'. Provide an introductory strategy (for a partially integrated approach).
or:
2.3 For the next target. 'X', provide a relevant context through an appropriate strategy (a stand-alone approach).

Step 3:
3.1 Develop the context and necessary knowledge through, for example, a demonstration, a display, a television programme, a visit, or a discussion.
3.2 Introduce the scientific investigation/experimentation in an appropriate way according to the degree of control or freedom required (for example, a guided investigation or a problem to solve).
3.3 Through questioning and discussion during and after the activity, check on children's developing knowledge and skills base and their construction of understanding.

Pre- and early Key Stage I (nursery and reception classes)

Step 1: At pre- and early KS1, the children should be given opportunities to ask questions, and be involved in focused explorations using first-hand experiences. Their understandings should be related to familiar home and school contexts. Very simple scientific vocabulary could be introduced to name and describe the world around them and themselves as living things.

In *Experimental and Investigative Science (Sc1)*, they could be asked to explore using appropriate senses to obtain evidence and communicate their explorations orally and in pictures.

In *Life Processes and Living Things (Sc2)*, they could be introduced to humans as organisms by looking at themselves and their bodies and naming the main external parts (e.g. hand, head, eyes, and so on).

Step 2: Start from topics which are immediately relevant to the children, and without the constraints of subject boundaries. Particularly useful strategies include stories and rhymes. For example, with a topic on 'Ourselves', the children could listen to the story *Funny Bones* by Janet and Alan Ahlberg and sing the song 'Dem Bones, Dem Bones'. They could then play a game like 'Simon Says' to focus on naming the different parts of their own bodies.

Step 3: Experiences can be provided in which the children are encouraged to observe carefully and notice similarities between things, ask questions which may lead to simple investigations, make simple predictions and suggest some simple explanations for things. For example, in the case of 'Ourselves', they could count how many legs, eyes, noses, etc., each of them has and develop an appreciation of the similarities between them all. They could then use what they know to predict how many legs, eyes, etc., a child in story will have. Looking at eye colour and hair colour and foot size introduces differences between them. Can they predict what colour eyes or hair the child will have? Draw a picture of their child and compare them.

Key Stage 1 (Years 1 and 2)

Step 1: At KS1, the Programmes of Study indicate that the children should be working towards asking questions, focused exploration and directed investigation. They should use simple secondary sources as well as first-hand experiences and also IT skills. Their ideas should be related to relevant contexts as well as to the evidence provided. They should communicate orally and in other ways, and health and safety aspects should be considered.

In *Experimental and Investigative Science (Sc1)* they could be encouraged to turn an idea into a simple investigation. This might involve making comparisons, collecting evidence by observing and measuring, and communicating their findings by drawing pictures and writing short accounts of what they did.

In *Materials and Their Properties (Sc3)* the children could investigate how different materials (paper, plastics, fabrics, and so on) behave under different conditions (dry, wet, stretched, compressed, etc.).

Step 2: Start from topics that the children can see as relevant and which can be explored using first-hand and simple secondary sources within school, home and the local community. For example, with the topic 'Shopping' a visit to a local supermarket can be a relevant starting point.

Step 3: Experiences should be provided in which the children are encouraged to observe carefully, ask questions leading to simple investigations, make simple predictions and suggest some simple explanations for things. For example, they could investigate how bags made from different materials (paper, cloth, plastic, etc.) behave when used to carry different kinds of shopping (heavy potatoes or damp frozen foods). Results could be recorded in a table, and an account of what was done and found could be prepared and presented to other children. Some simple data handling can be done by carrying out a survey of members of the family to find out where they prefer to shop.

Lower Key Stage 2 (Years 3 and 4)

Step 1: The Programmes of Study indicate that the younger Key Stage 2 children should be working towards asking questions related more closely to their experiences in science. They should be focusing their explorations and investigations to acquire scientific knowledge, understanding and skills, using simple secondary sources as well as first-hand experiences and also IT skills. Their ideas should be related to relevant contexts, particularly themselves and their environment, in an attempt to explain and interpret familiar phenomena. Communication in a variety of ways should be developed, and health and safety aspects considered.

In *Experimental and Investigative Science (Sc1)* they could be encouraged to turn ideas suggested to them into investigations. They should work through the processes of planning, selecting appropriate equipment, deciding what to control and change, and testing in a fair way. Their findings and conclusions could be explained in terms of prior experiences and existing knowledge and understanding.

In *Physical Processes (Sc4)* knowledge about 'Forces and Motion' could be used to plan and carry out of a fair test.

Step 2: Start from topics with a science focus (in this case 'Moving Around') which can be investigated through first-hand and secondary sources. For example, they could plan and carry out an investigation to answer the question, 'How can we make the toy car go further across the floor?'

Step 3: Sequential planning, accuracy in use of equipment, detailed observation for the purposes of comparison and careful recording of results should all be part of the experiences. Drawing on their results, they could produce an explanation that may lead to further investigation. For example, 'Does the weight of the toy car matter?'

Older Key Stage 2 (Years 5 and 6)

Step 1: The Programmes of Study indicate that the older Key Stage 2 children should be working towards turning their own questions and ideas into forms that can be investigated to acquire scientific knowledge, understanding and skills. They should use a range of secondary sources as well as first-hand experiences, as well as using IT skills. They need to relate their ideas to relevant contexts and explain and interpret familiar phenomena. How science has influenced human development should be considered. The collection and weighing of evidence to test scientific ideas should be introduced. Their skills at communicating in a variety of ways should be further refined. Health and safety aspects should begin to include the idea of risk assessment.

In *Experimental and Investigative Science (Sc1)* they could be encouraged to turn their own ideas into investigations by working through the processes of planning, selecting appropriate equipment, deciding what to control and change, and testing in a fair way; findings should be analysed for patterns, and conclusions could be explained in terms of prior experiences and existing knowledge and understanding.

In *Physical Processes (Sc4)*, as part of a topic on 'Light', knowledge and experience about sources and reflectors of light and how light travels in straight lines would be supplemented by using secondary sources for ideas.

Step 2: Start from topics with a science focus (in this case 'Light') which can be investigated through first-hand and secondary sources; for example, they could plan and carry out an investigation to answer the question, 'What causes shadows?'

Step 3: As with the younger Key Stage 2 pupils, sequential planning, accuracy in use of equipment, detailed observation for the purposes of comparison and careful recording of results should all be part of the experience. Drawing on their results, looking for patterns and explaining what they find are important outcomes; choosing for themselves how to communicate their findings to others and suggesting how conclusions may lead to further ideas for investigation are equally important. For example, investigating shadow sticks and sundials could be related to the movement of the Earth around the Sun and the cause of day and night. Investigating transparent, translucent and opaque materials can lead to ideas about what light can and cannot pass through.

Summing up

In this chapter, we have discussed two of the aspects of policy implementation which may require support from you as science coordinator: guidance on planning; and support with structuring classroom experiences appropriately. Some difficulties which you might anticipate and plan for include:

- how to guide and support teachers who want to do what they have always been doing;
- monitoring implementation at the classroom level to ensure that what is planned on paper is translated into practice.

Some suggestions to help with these problems were provided in earlier chapters. In the next section of this book we will return to how you can monitor the science education in your school for quality.

Part four　Monitoring for quality

Chapter 11

Monitoring and evaluating the science curriculum

Introduction

There are many opportunities for science activity in the primary classroom. The teacher's task is to plan for and help the children to use such opportunities to good effect. You, as the coordinator, will need to monitor and evaluate what opportunities are being provided in classrooms to ensure that effective teaching and learning in science is taking place. Only by doing so can you plan for improvement. Monitoring and evaluating the teaching and learning throughout your school will allow you to identify the strengths and weaknesses within the teaching and learning process. This evidence will then feed into your future action plans and ensure efficient management and use of resources. This should lead to an overall improvement in standards.

Most headteachers visit classrooms on a regular basis, although few carry out structured monitoring of practices and evaluation of outcomes in order to determine curricular strengths and weaknesses. This is something that is, invariably, left to curriculum coordinators. This is an important task, but you may find that establishing a procedure which is both manageable and effective is not easy.

Think about:
- the quality of the teaching of science throughout the school;
- the progress and achievements of all pupils in science;
- the extent to which the clear targets and expectations are being set and met.

Effective monitoring and evaluation can only take place if you have an established policy for science, with a clear set of aims and targets to be achieved, and schemes of work which identify issues of progression. These provide the basis for the evidence you will collect and the comparisons you can make. Developing the school's policy for science and translating it into practice were discussed in detail in Chapters 9 and 10. In the discussion which follows, we assume that documents of this nature exist in some form in your school.

In this chapter we will look at how, as the science coordinator, you can approach your monitoring and evaluation role and consider some aspects related to curriculum, planning and assessment which you will need to think about.

A model for monitoring and evaluating teaching and learning

Science 5–16: A Statement of Policy (DES, 1985) identified ten principles for good practice for planning and supporting teaching and learning in science. These criteria serve as a useful checklist for you when monitoring teaching and learning in science throughout your school.

DES (1985) criteria for good practice:
- breadth
- balance
- relevance
- differentiation
- equal opportunities
- continuity
- progression
- links across the curriculum
- teaching methods and approaches
- assessment

FIG 11.1
A model for monitoring and
evaluation

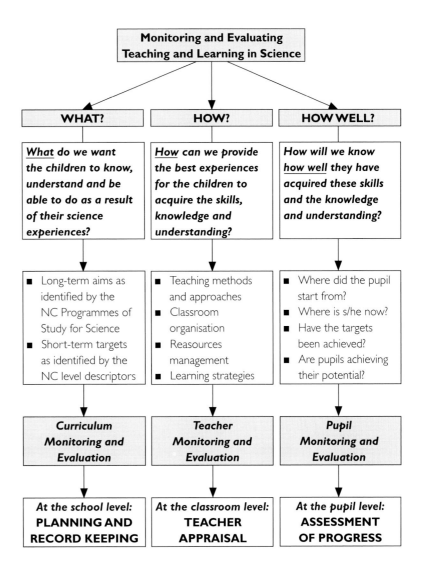

Whether you are reviewing the school's policy statement for science, looking at schemes and detailed planning, or looking at practice at the classroom level, you could use these ten criteria as a checklist to begin your thinking.

A more structured approach to monitoring and evaluating teaching and learning in science throughout your school is to use the evaluation model shown above in Figure 11.1. This model incorporates the ten criteria within the three stands of evaluation.

When thinking about teaching and learning in science, the central questions for teachers are:

- What is to be taught?
- How is it to be taught?
- What outcomes will be expected?

As the science coordinator, when you monitor and evaluate what is happening and the learning taking place, these questions change to:

- What is being taught? Is it meeting the National Curriculum and/or school policy requirements?
- How is it being taught? Are the most suitable and effective methods being used?
- What are the children achieving? Are they making progress and achieving the highest standards possible?

This means you need to think about the science curriculum itself and the planning to deliver that curriculum, the methods and approaches your colleagues choose, and the assessment process and how evidence is used. You will then need to decide what you, as the coordinator, need to do next to support colleagues to improve practice.

The what? — monitoring and evaluating the science curriculum

It is important that you monitor the science curriculum for several reasons. You need to ensure that the science education being provided for children is as effective as possible. You can then use the evidence to plan what support and staff development is needed by teachers to make them more effective. This evidence can then feed into the school development plan.

Monitoring and evaluating the science curriculum is very much related to planning at both school and class level. We will return to this later in this chapter (see pp. 141).

The how? — monitoring and evaluating the science teaching

How to offer science experience to children is not constrained by the National Curriculum Order. There is no requirement that science should be taught in a particular way, to use a particular method, or to employ a particular teaching strategy. These decisions are left to the teachers themselves, since no one organisational model or teaching method is likely to be equally appropriate to all classrooms or teachers. Schools are allowed to organise work to suit their children, teachers and circumstances on condition that National Curriculum requirements are met.

Monitoring and evaluating teaching will be returned to in more detail in Chapter 12.

The how well? — monitoring and evaluating the science learning

The third strand in the monitoring and evaluation model is how well the pupils have performed in science. When discussing assessment in science, Harlen (1983) suggested:

 Assessing children's educational development is an essential part of fostering that development, of teaching, so that both short and long-term planning of activities can match the stages reached and provide optimum opportunities for further learning. (p. 3)

This emphasises the complex interrelationship of curriculum planning, teaching methods and approaches and the assessment of outcomes. It also reinforces the importance of you, as coordinator, having an overview of the whole complex process.

We will return to assessment, and the related issues of record keeping and reporting, in Chapter 13.

Monitoring and evaluating the science curriculum

The starting point for monitoring the science curriculum is the policy statement and scheme of work. All staff should have been involved in the drawing up of these documents in consultation with the science coordinator, and they are useful reference points for you when monitoring and evaluating the science curriculum. They should relate closely to other school policy documents, such as that for assessment, marking, record-keeping and so on.

> *Check:*
> - What does the science policy statement and the related documents tell you about the science curriculum? Look for evidence of:
>   - breadth;
>   - balance;
>   - continuity; and,
>   - progression

Breadth

All pupils in your school should be experiencing a broad science curriculum. This means that they will be learning about science both as a body of knowledge and as a way of thinking and working. The opportunities provided by teachers need to support the development of skills needed for exploring, investigating and experimenting. They also need to support the construction of understanding of living things, materials, forces, energy, and the Earth and its place in Space.

> *Check:*
> - Does the policy statement and the scheme of work cover science in a broad way? Are all children, at all ages, being given opportunities to learn about the world around them in line with the National Curriculum Order for Science?
> - Look for evidence that the various aspects of Sc1, Sc2, Sc3 and Sc4 are being covered at the appropriate key stages.

Balance

All pupils are required to study science throughout their school lives. The programme designed to achieve this in your school needs to reflect a balance in the major components of science and also make provision for all pupils to have access to these components. The National Curriculum Order for Science selects *Life Processes and Living Things, Materials and Their Properties* and *Physical Processes* to represent the major components of conceptual knowledge and defines the skills to be practised in *Experimental and Investigative Science.* Each should be given a fair and reasonable representation in activities.

Particularly in primary schools, where many colleagues have little or no expertise in science, there is a risk that this balance is not addressed. Teachers may find it easier to teach about the natural world rather than the physical world. They may also find it preferable to minimise practical and investigative work in favour of teaching facts. Through conscious planning, you must ensure that equal weighting is given to the development of skills as well as to the acquisition of knowledge and understanding in science. One of the things you will need to do as the coordinator is monitor whether or not this balance is being provided, not only within the school programme for science, but also in the classrooms themselves.

Check:
- Does the school programme/scheme of work for science reflect this balance across Sc1, Sc2, Sc3 and Sc4?
- Is each aspect receiving the appropriate weighting in terms of time and resources?
- Are teachers providing the balance in the classroom in line with the aims and targets of the school scheme?
- Look for evidence of both physical and natural science activities being provided by each teacher as appropriate to the Key Stage requirements.
- Also look for Sc1 activities in each class programme.

Continuity

The primary school phase of children's education is very varied. If what has been achieved at each stage is not to be lost, coordinators need to establish links between the stages to ensure continuity. Many schools have structures in place to aid transition from one phase of education to the next. These are often concerned with reducing children's worries about such transitions, but that alone does not bring about continuity.

Some strategies to reduce children's apprehension which you might try are:

■ Visits by older pupils in the infant, first or primary school to the next school they will attend. They could be involved in some science activities while they are at the same time becoming familiar with their new environment.

■ Visits by pupils in the first class of the new school the pupils will be attending to work alongside the older infant, first or primary school pupils, perhaps in a peer-tutoring capacity. This can work well for practical science activities.

■ Science fairs, involving all the schools in the area, with common themes or investigations so that children can talk to one another about what they are doing and share experiences.

To ensure continuity in science experiences you might consider joint staff meetings to share ideas, explore common issues such as planning, record-keeping and assessment and, perhaps, organise some joint in-service training.

Progression

In your role as coordinator, you will come across two uses of the word *progression*. First, there is progression in relation to a course or programme of study for science, whether planned for a group such as a class or a year group and covering a long period of time. This kind of progression generally relates to the long-term goals when planning. The second use describes progression in experiences planned for individuals in order to develop their skills, knowledge and understanding in science. This type of progression is more closely related to the short-term, specific learning and behavioural targets when planning at the specific activity or lesson level. The two are related, although not interchangeable. Schemes or programmes of study in science for the whole school should support increasing levels of skill, knowledge and understanding in science by individual children. This is generally what is thought of as progression. While it is likely to be your task, as the coordinator, to provide the former, it will be for individual colleagues to interpret the scheme and match specific experiences to the needs of the children in their class.

While matching experiences to the needs of individuals in order to ensure progression is generally thought to be both feasible and desirable, it is no easy task. If a teacher cannot do it, it may seem to reflect a problem with the teacher rather than with the ideas under study themselves. Such difficulties are likely to require your help to resolve them.

There are certain assumptions that underpin matching and progression through the learning experience which you will need to think about. First, the notion of progression assumes that the level of demand of a learning experience can be assessed reasonably accurately, Second, it assumes that the level of development of children can be assessed with equal accuracy. Finally, there is the assumption that learning experiences can be designed to match these two and, consequently, prove effective. However, the time and effort to do this would seem to outweigh the outcomes, since children, contexts and subject matter all vary. Children do not come to new learning experiences with empty heads. Judgments about how meaningful and demanding any task is will depend upon knowledge of the whole learning situation and the prior knowledge and experiences of the individual pupils. Their performance on activities will change according to contexts and emotions — children do not operate constantly at the same uniform level. Any prediction of their future performance can, at best, be no more than tentative, since it will be affected by numerous other factors, such as linguistic and mathematical demand, social interaction skills and general physical and emotional state. In other words, since such matching can only ever be loose and approximate, your time and effort as the coordinator would seem to be better spent on more general and global strategies for individual, group and class progression.

> **Check:**
> - Does the school programme/scheme for science reflect progression in the general and global sense?
> - Are learning experiences revisited at different points in a child's primary school career?
> - Do all teachers have an overview of the school scheme so that they know what has gone before for the different aspects of science, and can then build on what has been done previously?
> - How does the school's record-keeping system allow information related to progression to be recorded and shared?

Planning science experiences

In the past, teachers have been able to plan in isolation and classrooms have functioned with relative independence. Since the introduction of the National Curriculum, this is no longer feasible. Planning for learning in science is something which encompasses the school as a whole in planning curricula.

> **Think about:**
> One of the things you will need to do as the coordinator is to encourage your colleagues to talk about how they plan and why they use particular approaches. Some questions you might use to begin discussions include:
> - How are different levels of planning coordinated throughout the school?
> - What are the different starting points with your colleagues for discussions about planning?
> - How do you, as the coordinator, plan your science teaching at the classroom level?
>
> The school policy and programme for science can be a good starting point. Blank planning sheets can also be useful.

You are likely to find that planning what to teach in science is no longer the problem for your colleagues that it was in the past. The National Curriculum requirements in this respect are listed in the Programmes of Study. These are translated into learning and behavioural targets in the level desciptors and these can then be used for assessment purposes. If you have in place a whole school programme for science, then your next step will be to monitor the translation of that general plan into detailed planning at the classroom level.

Of particular importance to you will be the school's approach to planning. If there is a clear planning policy in operation, with standardised planning sheets, then your task will be made somewhat easier. By monitoring teachers' planning files (or whatever system is used to store the planning sheets), you can check that breadth, balance, continuity and progression are being planned for. Planning in relation to translating the science policy into practice was discussed in Part 3.

Summing up

In this chapter, we have discussed some of the general issues which you will have to think about as the science coordinator in connection with monitoring and evaluating effectiveness of the science curriculum. Some difficulties you might anticipate and plan for include:
- how the monitoring and evaluation follow from the science policy and its implementation;
- how you can ensure an effective match between the general school aims and the specific classroom targets.

We will discuss monitoring and evaluation at the classroom level in the next chapter.

| Chapter 12 | Monitoring and evaluating science teaching |

Introduction

Having evaluated the science curriculum structure for your school, your next task as the coordinator is to begin to focus on how this curriculum is implemented at the classroom level. This means first looking for evidence that teachers are providing children with experiences in science which are not only in line with the broad curriculum requirements but are also delivered in the most appropriate and effective ways possible to ensure meaningful learning with understanding. This evidence can then be used by you to plan how to deal with the weaknesses and inconsistencies, as well as building on the strengths.

Monitoring science teaching

What will you be looking for when you are monitoring and evaluating teachers' practices at the classroom level? You will need to think about:
- *the learning environment each teacher creates:* organisation of the classroom; organisation of the children themselves; the resources used; the displays created;
- *the learning experiences for science provided for the class:* translating the formal aims of the science curriculum into a topic web; scheme of work; lesson or activity plans;

cross curricular integration; teaching methods and approaches;

■ *that specific targets for the experiences meet individual needs:*

does planning reflect thinking about relevance, differentiation, and equal opportunities?

The DES (1985) policy statement for science identifies some criteria for good practice which are particularly relevant to your task of monitoring and evaluating the teaching of science in individual classrooms. These are:

■ relevance;
■ differentiation;
■ equal opportunities; and,
■ links across the curriculum.

Relevance

One aim of science education is to prepare pupils for life in a scientific and technological society. Children need to appreciate that science is a human activity which satisfies needs. The kinds of need which come to mind most readily tend to be those associated with the application of scientific knowledge through technology. Here, children can be made aware that this involves difficult decisions which may have consequences that are beneficial, benign or detrimental.

At the same time, as teachers we should not neglect the other needs which science satisfies, personal needs like satisfying curiosity and the need to understand the biophysical world. This is what makes it relevant but this relevance may not always be made explicit by teachers, and you should look for it when you monitor teaching.

Check:
There are a number of ways in which your colleagues can make science education explicitly relevant. When you discuss planning or observe teaching, look for evidence of:
■ Drawing on the immediate and everyday experiences of children to teach science through contexts to which children can relate.
■ Putting people back into science by using examples from the history of science to show science as a human activity, engaged in and enjoyed by men *and* women.

- Looking at science in society, in particular in industry and commerce.
- Exploring some controversial issues related to science, technology and the environment, such as pollution or over-fishing the oceans, to weigh issues and question actions.

Differentiation

Differentiation means different things to different teachers. In essence, the intellectual and practical demands made in science teaching should be suited to the abilities of children. In other words, their prior experiences and abilities should be taken into account when planning new experiences. In the extreme, differentiation can involve a totally separate education for some children. More commonly it can involve streaming or grouping by ability within a class. In a more general sense, almost anything can be differentiated — the tasks and activities, the expectations or outcomes, the resources used, the nature of the support from or interaction with the teacher. In their planning for science, teachers should be providing for children's individual needs and differences, and when you are monitoring their teaching you should be looking for evidence of appropriate differentiation. Some of your colleagues may use open-ended activities in science. Such an approach allows children to interpret tasks and activities at different levels. However, such tasks must be planned with the other criteria for good practice in mind, particularly those of breadth, balance, continuity and progression in line with the school's science policy.

Check:
- Does the teacher's planning indicate awareness of the different needs of the pupils, both in terms of Sc1 and of Sc2, Sc3 or Sc4?
- Are tasks and activities being presented and supported at different levels in line with these needs?
- Are other forms of differentiation (e.g. resources or textual material) evident, as appropriate?

Differentiation in science may be an area which you feel could be the basis of a staff development session, since it is fundamental to effective teaching.

Equal opportunities

Teachers need to plan and teach science so that every child in the class has equal access to the experiences and can make progress in line with his or her potential, regardless of sex, race or ability. This criterion is one of the dimensions of the whole curriculum discussed in Chapter 8 (pages 99 to 101). As the coordinator, when you are monitoring and evaluating teaching you will need to check that this principle is being put into practice at the classroom level, both in teachers' planning and in the delivery.

Check:
■ Does the teacher seem to plan with equal opportunity in mind?
■ Are there any incidents where children are not being treated in line with the policy statement on equal opportunity?

Links across the curriculum

Science pervades all aspects of our lives and lends itself well to cross-curricular and integrated experiences, crossing traditional subject boundaries and using a wide range of skills. While science education can be planned to stand alone in the curriculum this does not have to be the case. A cross-curricular approach may be used to integrate experiences. One way to make the relevance of science more explicit is to take opportunities to link the science experiences to other areas of the curriculum and break down the compartmentalisation of subjects. This can be done even where science is taught as an independent subject all or some of the time.

Check:
When looking at planning or observing colleagues, ask:
■ Does the teacher take opportunities to link science to other areas of experience, as appropriate?
■ What opportunities are taken? What are missed?

This is also something which primary teachers are usually very good at doing and you are likely to find that during whole school or team planning sessions, your colleagues identify links across the curriculum very easily.

Teaching methods and approaches

Science involves the acquisition of mental and physical skills as well as procedural and conceptual knowledge and understanding. It should be taught in ways which enable both to develop. It is important that you recognise that there are many different teaching styles and ways of working. What might not work for you could work very well for someone else, and vice versa, so as the coordinator you need to be open-minded about the different methods and approaches possible.

In your monitoring role, you will also see a variety of learning situations — from individual and small group focused to large group and whole class activity — each of which may be appropriate to achieve different ends.

One factor your colleagues may be concerned about in relation to practical activities in science is class size. There are contrasting claims by policy makers and practitioners about the effects of class sizes on standards and levels of achievement. Ovens (1994) considered the research findings of science educators from around the world and concluded that,

> *The broader picture that emerges from evaluation of the findings of each research project is that smaller class sizes appear to contribute significantly to improvement in the kinds of children's learning tested, when teachers use the opportunities thus created.* (p. 2)

What appears to be important is how the teacher interacts with the children and how their achievements are assessed. In the context of science, larger class sizes reduce the time for observation of practical activity, discussion and questioning for each child.

When you monitor and evaluate the teaching methods and approaches being used, there are several things you need to consider. They include:
- the variety of teaching approaches for science;
- different ways of organising the classroom for science;

- the management of the children during science activities; and,
- The teacher's role during the science activities.

Teaching approaches

There are two main approaches. One is to develop a subject-based curriculum in which science is taught as a separate subject. The other is to work through integrated topics or themes. There are, of course, hybrids.

From your viewpoint as the coordinator, there are some advantages to using the subject-based approach. It is possible to plan a programme for science for the whole school which ensures progression in skills, knowledge and understanding through a continuous sequence of experiences from the Reception class to the oldest pupils. Such a programme avoids unnoticed duplication and significant omissions of experiences. It is also easy to monitor such a programme and to update and change it. It allows you to encourage particular teachers to focus on certain aspects of science within the programme according to their strengths and interests. When the programme is clearly structured in this way you can manage the resources more easily, avoiding several teachers wanting the same things at the same time. This also has economic advantages for your school, since resources need not be duplicated.

Inevitably, there are also several disadvantages of a subject-based approach which you will need to consider. The main one is the loss of spontaneity and flexibility. Such a curriculum may be divided into slots in which the children cannot spend longer than planned on tasks. This can limit opportunities for differentiation. At the same time, opportunities to link curricular experiences can be missed. However, it is possible to overcome these with careful planning.

The second approach is to plan the science through topics or themes. As with the first approach, there are advantages and disadvantages. A topic or thematic approach means you can encourage integrated learning experiences. It allows some freedom and flexibility, providing opportunities for the children to contribute personal interests and ideas, and also enabling the teacher to respond spontaneously to events which might be used as a starting point. It facilitates different ways of organising practical activities, particularly small group and individual work, which not only encourage communication and interaction, but may also reduce demands on resources. Finally, it can allow children to work at their own pace and level and supports a differentiated programme.

On the other hand, not every topic or theme will contain opportunities for science activities and this will be a major concern for you as the coordinator. Given that science is a core subject, it is unlikely that teachers can afford to spend a long time on a topic which does not include science. At the same time, there could be a lack of breadth, balance and continuity unless the programme for the whole school is planned cooperatively. If topics are being used like this, when you monitor teachers' planning and teaching you will need to ensure that all the appropriate elements of the Programmes of Study for Science are covered.

Check:
- Is the overall approach being used in line with school policy?
- Does what the teacher is planning and teaching match what is required in terms of the stage in the school's science programme, regardless of the approach being used?
- Is the work building on what has gone before and delivering appropriate new skills, knowledge and understanding?

Classroom organisation

There are a number of ways classrooms can be organised for teaching science. Some of your colleagues will prefer to have the whole class doing science at the same time. On occasions, this may be a more difficult way to organise science, since you could find it makes greater demands on resources. On other occasions, it is a good way to introduce new ideas and demonstrate procedures to everyone. It is also useful for reporting back, explaining or reiterating particular points. If whole class teaching is used in this way, furniture should be arranged to maximise involvement.

Often, as coordinator you will be encouraging your colleagues to allow children to work on science investigations in small groups. This is particularly appropriate when the equipment and resources are in short supply. Friendship groups can be a good starting point for practical activities as sharing and cooperation may be more easily facilitated. However, such groups will often be single-sex and there may be occasions when cooperation between the sexes is desirable. Friendship groups may also combine passive and active pupils so there will be occasions when other mixes are desirable. With this method of organisation the teacher still retains the option of having the whole class do science at the same time, either on the same or on a variety of different activities.

When children investigate and experiment as a group (as opposed to *in* a group), it can be more productive if they are assigned individual roles or special responsibilities. Initially, these are allocated by the teacher but, as the children gain confidence and competence, they might select who does what for themselves. For example, with a group of four older junior children one could be the chairperson for the session, leading the group, stating the details of the task or investigation and managing the working arrangements. A second child might be the secretary, who records the discussion, the ideas suggested, what the group feel or know about what they are working on and what results are collected. A third person might collect and put away the resources and equipment used. The final member might be responsible for deciding how and what is reported back to the whole class and for organising the presentation. All members of the group would be involved in contributing ideas and in carrying out the actual investigation. If the group was one which existed for any length of time, then the children would rotate the roles from week to week as they moved on to new investigations. Such a structure offers children real opportunities for developing interaction, communication skills and cooperative decision making.

Some teachers might decide to have children working individually or in pairs. In an ideal world, every child in the class would be able to carry out experiments and investigations, practice skills and manipulate scientific equipment individually or with a partner whenever they wished. However, this is seldom feasible but, if space allows, individual work can be supported using science areas. These areas may include:

- a three-dimensional display area which can be changed regularly;
- a clean area for activities which require mental work rather than physical action, such as reference skills and writing;
- an area where practical tasks can be carried out, such as working with water;
- a secure storage area for the sort of materials used in science but common to all classrooms, such as measuring equipment and containers;
- some access to a computer and appropriate science-focused software.

Such areas are likely to serve several purposes and will be used for activities other than science. The idea can be developed further in the science learning station or workstation.

Work stations are not a new idea. In the United States, they are common in many elementary schools and are particularly important for practical activities in subjects such as science. A learning station is a place where several children can work independently, using instructions and guidance and the resources for the activities located in the station. Learning stations can be established for any area of the curriculum or for cross-curricular topic work and are designed to support a differentiated approach to teaching and learning. Children may select which tasks they wish to do, the order in which they will do them and then work at them at their own rate.

At the learning station, the children will find a background display of posters and artefacts, books, pictures, slides and other resources relevant to the topic or theme, along with examples of children's own work and investigations. This would serve to orient minds towards the topic, focus attention and motivate. Children who are non-readers may listen to information, instructions, stories and poems on a tape recorder. The station would also hold an assortment of workcards or task sheets. These might include:

■ structured workcards or worksheets, suggesting things the children might explore and investigate, with some guidance on how to start their investigations;

■ planning sheets for investigations, to be completed by the individuals or groups to show the nature of the investigation and how it would be carried out;

■ plan–do–review sheets to be completed by individuals to indicate what his or her contribution to the investigation was and their evaluation of their learning experiences;

■ support, extension and challenge sheets to be used as needed.

A record book is kept at the learning station for the children to record when they use the workstation, for how long, what they did and which cards or sheets they completed.

Simple instructions, on display above the station, tell the children how to use it, how many children should be there at any one time, how to use equipment and deal with missing items, breakages, and so on. Once established, particularly with older pupils, the children themselves can take some responsibility for restocking it. With younger pupils, an adult may help them do it.

> *Check:*
> ■ How is the teacher organising the class? Is it the most appropriate method to achieve the learning targets of the lesson? What is her/his role with the method of organisation chosen?
> ■ If the teacher is working with the whole class as one group, what kind of involvement is expected on the part of individuals? Are the children seated appropriately for the purpose?
> ■ If children are working in groups, is it genuinely group interaction? Have children clear tasks or roles within the group? Are they all participating?
> ■ What are the resource implications of the chosen approach? Are resources being accessed efficiently and safely? How demanding is resourcing on the teacher's time?

Class management

There are three things the teacher will need to consider when thinking about class management. These are:

- *Safety:* Science investigations in the classroom need to be carried out safely.
- *Furniture:* Few primary schools are likely to have a dedicated science room or laboratory.
- *Resources:* Whichever storage system is used, a wise teacher will organise them so that the children can access and return them themselves.

These will be considered in Chapter 14, when discussing the management of resources as part of your role as a coordinator.

Check:
Safety:
- Are there clear traffic routes through the classroom?
- Are safety glasses needed for some activities?
- If pupils are using computers and electronic sensors, are appropriate safety precautions taken e.g. using a circuit breaker?
- Is the teacher familiar with local and national safety regulations?

Furniture:
- Are surfaces washable or, at least, covered to protect their surfaces and are they free of all unnecessary objects?
- Is there a suitable place for a computer?

Resources:
- Are all the basic materials needed by the class or group for the task in hand available?
- Is there access to a range of common materials, such as paper, coloured pencils, measuring instruments, scissors, glue, and containers?
- Is there sufficient variety to allow children's ideas for investigations to be developed?

The teacher's role

As a general rule, children are more motivated to engage in activities when given some choice in what they do and variety in ways of doing it. They may also learn well from first-hand experience, through interaction with others and through necessity. The teacher's role in this process will vary, depending upon the abilities and needs of the children and the nature of the experiences. At any one time, the teacher may take on one of several roles, and you will need to identify what his or her role is in the science classroom, since each achieves different ends.

Check:
What is the teacher's role in the classroom?
- *Leader:* encouraging discussion, guiding thinking, supporting recall of prior knowledge, and providing knowledge, information, instructions and guidance.
- *Questioner:* using key questions to focus attention on important aspects of the task, direct observations, encourage prediction and inferencing, applications of ideas in new contexts, and evaluation and hypothesising, helping raise questions for exploration and investigation.
- *Assessor:* appraising ideas and explanations put forward during discussion, questions raised for investigation and experimentation, and feasibility and safety of ideas for practical work.
- *Challenger:* using tasks which encourage children to practise parts of or the full process of investigating ideas, including planning, collecting and weighing evidence.
- *Observer:* watching as children generate ideas, explore and investigate, building a picture of the child's thinking so that future work can be planned.

A model for monitoring and evaluating teaching

One of the things you must decide is the best way to collect this necessary information. None of the methods you identify will be effective without the cooperation of your colleagues. Consequently you must first discuss with your headteacher what you are wanting to do and why, and gain his or her support. Then, explain clearly to staff what you would like to do, and how important it is for the long term-goal of supporting and improving science education throughout the school. Since the last thing you want to do is make teachers feel threatened by your actions, you will need to use tact and diplomacy. Emphasise that the information collected will not be used to criticise them in any way or for any other purpose than planning what support might be useful and what resources might be needed.

What methods are available to you to collect information?

- An observation schedule of this nature is of use in all kinds of situations in schools — for observation of lessons by coordinators (whether of teachers or students), as a self-evaluation checksheet by individual teachers to monitor their own practices, by headteachers or senior staff for formal appraisal purposes.
- You could suggest designing your own school version of the schedule for staff to use. Colleagues can then contribute their own ideas and include what they feel is important in the schedule, according to the particular context and needs of your school.
- If you are in partnership with any local universities for teacher training purposes, look at copies of their schedules for evaluating students' competences. They might provide further ideas for discussion.

Think about:

- looking at planning files or folders to check aims and targets;
- talking with teachers about their own evaluations of their science teaching;
- talking with children about what they have been doing in science;
- sampling children's work;
- carrying out some structured classroom observation of colleagues.

In practice, your choice will be determined by how much time is available to you as the coordinator for the task. If your headteacher has been able to build into the school budget expenditure on supply cover for you to fulfil this role, then options like observing colleagues at work are feasible. On the other hand, if release from your own class is not possible, then more indirect means, like looking at planning and talking with colleagues over lunch, might be all you can do for the moment. You can, however, identify this as a budget priority for the future.

If you are able to observe colleagues at work in their classrooms, it may be useful to have a structured observational schedule which can focus your attention on a standard set of actions and procedures which apply to everyone and which all teachers would agree are elements of good practice. A schedule which you can enlarge and use for this purpose is given in Figure 12.1 (p. 161).

Summing up

In this chapter we have explored some of the characteristics of effective teaching in science in line with the government's criteria which you will need to monitor and evaluate as the science coordinator. We have described ways in which you might collect information about your colleagues' teaching and suggested some things which you will need to think about. Some difficulties which you might anticipate and plan for include:

- the cooperation of your colleagues in this process will be essential if monitoring is going to be effective;

FIG 12.1
An evaluation schedule which can be used to observe colleagues or for self-evaluation

Topic:	Class Teacher:	Dates:
Sc1 Learning Targets:	Sc2, 3 or 4 Learning Targets:	
Structure of Lesson/Experience:	Relevant Cross-curricular Links:	
	Teaching and Learning Strategies used:	
Class Organisation and Management:	Resources Used:	
	Safety Notes:	
Assessment Targets:	Any Other Points:	

© Falmer Press Ltd

- you will need to ensure that teachers do not feel threatened by the notion of them being evaluated in this way;
- classrooms are complex places and so evidence from a variety of sources should be used to construct a picture of practice.

Of course, monitoring and evaluating what teaching has occurred and what learning opportunities have been provided for the children is not the same as knowing what has actually been learned. Your role in this respect is the focus of the next chapter.

Chapter 13   Monitoring and evaluating science learning

Introduction

The third strand to the evaluation model introduced in
Chapter 11 (pp. 138–141) was that concerned with
assessment of progress — *How well are the children doing?*
As the coordinator, you will need to spend some time
monitoring and evaluating the effectiveness of what has been
planned and taught in science. In other words, you will need
to address the question, *What are the children learning in
science?* Such assessment is an important part of any
effective curriculum for any teacher, and very much part of
your responsibility as the coordinator. It will involve you in
making judgments based on clear evaluation criteria and
using evidence collected in a variety of ways.

The procedure of monitoring and evaluating the effectiveness
of the science curriculum and its delivery by your colleagues
is no different to teachers' own evaluation of their
effectiveness when they monitor children's progress. They are
constantly judging what children do. In the first instance,
this is likely to be based on impressions and an experienced
teacher can quickly sense when things are going well and the
atmosphere is conducive to learning. However, there are
times when such judgments must be more objective. You can
work in the same way.

Think about:

- Why are you monitoring and evaluating the learning that is taking place in science?
- How will you carry out this monitoring?
- How will you evaluate the information collected?
- How will you act on that information?

It is these elements of evaluation which we will be looking at in this chapter, in connection with your role as the coordinator.

Purposes

Teachers need to be seen to be effective by their colleagues, pupils and parents. Appraisal methods and OFSTED inspection procedures judge teachers' choice of methods, approaches and strategies according to their effectiveness in delivering the planned curriculum as perceived by the appraiser or the inspector. Such effectiveness is usually determined by looking at the evidence gathered through the assessment process: how well pupils have performed, what progress they have made and what has been achieved as a result of experiences provided by their teachers.

Think about:

When, as coordinator, you are monitoring and evaluating the learning that has taken place in colleagues' classrooms, what are you looking for evidence of? Think about:

- Is the science curriculum planned for the whole school effective in terms of breadth, balance, continuity and progression in children's learning in science?
- Is each teacher delivering what is planned?
- Are the children developing skills, knowledge and understanding in science in line with their needs and abilities through a relevant and differentiated programme which provides equal opportunities and makes links across the curriculum?
- Are the teaching methods and approaches the teacher has chosen to use effective?
- Is the way the teacher is organising and managing the learning environment for science effective?
- Does the teacher have an overall picture of each child's progress and achievements in science?

One of the main differences in purpose between yourself as the coordinator gathering evidence for evaluation purposes, and teachers doing the same thing relates to the audience. In the case of the teachers, they are their own audience. For you, with your focus on monitoring and evaluating learning across the school, the audience may be all staff, and possibly governors and parents. As such you need to use objective methods in line with clear aims and criteria.

Methods

Just as there are a number of ways in which, teachers assess children's learning, as coordinator there are a number of ways you can evaluate the learning taking place in science. The strategies you might use as a coordinator are no different to those you would use with your own class and they vary in quality and objectivity.

Think about:
What are the main evaluation strategies you can use? Perhaps you need to talk with the assessment coordinator and plan a discussion during a staff meeting to explore your colleagues' ideas. Think about:

- observing children as they work;
- talking with them about their work;
- looking at their workbooks and folders;
- looking at classroom displays;
- looking at school records;
- talking with teachers about children's progress and achievements;
- looking at their portfolios of achievement;
- looking at performance profiles as reflected by test results;
- involving children in some self-evaluation;
- using questionnaires to teachers and/or pupils.

Find out how teachers collect evidence of learning, and how they sample, select and annotate work. Draw on these various sources of evidence for your own monitoring and evaluation exercise.

Record-keeping

Once you have begun to focus in detail on the assessment of children's learning and the effectiveness of curriculum planning and teaching methods and approaches, you will rapidly begin to recognise the importance of an effective record-keeping system for science. Record-keeping is an aspect of communication which has an important role to play in effective teaching and learning. Teachers need to record not only the experiences planned and provided for children but also the outcomes of those experiences in terms of what children have learned, acquired or achieved.

Think about:
Your school will need to maintain some sort of record of each child's progress in science for several reasons:
- In a busy classroom so much is happening that it is not possible for the teacher to remember everything about each child's achievements in all subjects.
- By bringing together various pieces of evidence and bits of information collected over time and in different ways, the teacher can begin to see patterns in a pupil's progress and build a profile of development.
- Such a record allows the teacher to spot areas of strengths and weaknesses and this aids planning.
- Such records aid the communication process, supporting discussion between teachers as well as with the children.

What does the school currently do? Is it effective?

The responsibility for designing an efficient record-keeping system is likely to have been yours, as the science coordinator, and you will need to monitor its use and effectiveness across the school. However, you will need to keep in mind that a record-keeping system is not an end in itself. It can only guide and support planning and assessment procedures.

The 3Ms principle (Harlen, 1983) is a good one to follow. Records should be:
- *Minimal:* providing only the information needed by those maintaining and using them.
- *Manageable:* record-keeping should be neither arduous nor time-consuming; it should support planning, teaching and assessment, not be at the expense of these processes.
- *Meaningful:* record-keeping should be seen by teachers as an integral part of the teaching–learning process and show progression and continuity in the science experiences and achievements of pupils.

> If there is already a record-keeping system in place for science, does it fit these principles? How are your colleagues using it? Should it be reviewed and improved?

As the coordinator, you will need to ensure that the record-keeping system for science can be used with consistency throughout the school and encourages class teachers to indicate:

- the science experiences provided for pupils (e.g. an activity record which can apply to the whole class, perhaps detailed class planning sheets);
- the children's responses to the provision (e.g. a personal record applying to each child, with the supporting evidence to substantiate judgments, perhaps a portfolio of work);
- the achievements of each child over time (e.g. a summative record, perhaps completed at the end of each topic, term or year).

Think about:
What types of records can be maintained?

Formative record-keeping supports the day-to-day routines of the classroom. It includes:

- summaries of experiences provided to the whole class which focus on what broad activities have been offered to the children;
- criterion-based checklists, which focus on what the children should know, understand and be able to do;
- scores or ratings, based on teacher's marking of work and assessment tests given;
- free comments, perhaps in a notebook, reflecting observations and discussions.

Summative record-keeping summarises each child's progress on the basis of all the evidence provided. It includes:

- recording grids or wheels, which can relate directly to the National Curriculum Order for Science;
- report forms with criterion-based summaries.

Reviewing and improving records

In your monitoring and evaluation role you will need to review the record-keeping system from the point of view of teaching and learning, and it is important to remember the interconnected nature of planning, teaching, assessment and record-keeping. A good recording system cannot make up for deficiencies in the planning, teaching or assessment procedures. Records can only ever reflect the information gathered but all too often they can develop a life of their own and acquire a permanence which can disable good practice. To balance this, you will need to review the form and content of records regularly and, if necessary, revise the system in the light of other changes and developments in the school.

Changes include:
- those imposed from outside as curriculum orders change;
- changes in staffing;
- introducing new approaches or resources;
- changes in the schools' general reporting mechanisms.

Reviewing and revising the record-keeping system for science is likely to follow from a review of the school's general record-keeping policy and is very much a whole staff activity, although you are likely to have the responsibility of interpreting it. Since all teachers are to use the records, they should be given the opportunity to be involved in the review.

Think about:
As the coordinator, you will need to structure the review of the record-keeping policy so that it focuses upon certain things:

Details in the records:
- Do the records enable teachers to identify all of the key areas (skills, knowledge and understanding) in science, in line with the National Curriculum requirements and the school's science policy statement?
- Is the information about each area of experience in sufficient detail to show each child's progress and development?

Completion of the records:
- How often are the records to be completed?
- Who must complete the records at these times?
- Is this too often / too infrequently / about right?
- Is there a set of notes or guidelines available on completing and using the records, defining terms and identifying who does what and when?

(This may be part of the broader school policy document on record keeping.)

Use of the records:

- Who uses the records and why?
- Where are they located?
- Are they secure?
- Are there opportunities for consultation about records?

Inclusions with the records:

- Are test results presented in a clear and informative way?
- Are copies of tasks, tests and SATs included in the record folder or portfolio?
- What other information is needed in the record folder or portfolio?

Reporting progress and achievement to others

Effective reporting is not a simple process, nor is it something which will be dealt with only by you as the science coordinator. It should be part of a broader school policy, with each subject area contributing to the process. Good reporting requires a shared understanding of the basis on which the curriculum is planned, assessments are made, and the ways in which judgments about progress can be reported to relevant audiences. Since each of your colleagues will generally do her or his own reporting, you may need to give some guidance on how reporting in science can be made effective to ensure consistency across the school. Reporting on children's progress in science is an essential part of the progressive development of children's skills, knowledge and understanding in science. It also helps to shape the quality of the relationships teachers have with colleagues, parents and the children. It is also shaped by such relationships.

As the science coordinator, you may be asked to give feedback on children's learning and progress in science at any time, even for children not in your class, and so you need to encourage a system which provides you with information as well. When you discuss teachers' planning or work with them in their classrooms, you will need to encourage them to think about their use of reporting to different audiences for different purposes, and look for evidence that this is happening.

Who is receiving the report?

While teachers give informal feedback to children as they work or to parents when they visit the classroom, they need to report more formally on children's progress to a variety of audiences and for a variety of purposes. Each of these audiences has different needs in terms of the quantity and nature of the information reported to them. Reporting to parents orally or in writing in a way which does not meet their needs will affect the quality of the relationships with the parents. Similarly, giving colleagues information for which they have little use will devalue the importance of the assessment, recording and reporting process. A final point relates to the children themselves. Since the reports are about them, they should, as far as is possible and appropriate, be involved in the reporting process.

Think about:
During your discussions, encourage teachers to think about the needs of different audiences:
- parents or guardians (e.g. termly or yearly progress);
- other teachers taking the class (e.g. subject specialists taking the class, supply teachers, student teachers);
- other teachers in other schools (e.g. the next class teacher);
- other teachers in the schools (e.g. if the family moves to a new area, or when the class transfers);
- other professionals (e.g. an educational psychologist or counsellor working with the child);
- the children themselves.

Why give reports?

During discussions, encourage your colleagues to consider different reasons for reporting children's progress in science.

Think about:
- motivation (e.g. using constructive and positive feedback to children encourages achievement);
- clarification of needs (e.g. helps to involve parents in their child's education and strengthens home–school relationships;

- effective transfer (e.g. especially when associated with good records, saves time and effort);
- reflection by teachers (e.g. evaluation of learning experiences offered and progress made, aiding planning of ways forward);
- provision of support (e.g. progress reports on pupils with particular or special needs which require some additional action beyond the classroom).

When is reporting necessary?

You will need to make clear to your colleagues that here is no hard and fast rule about when reporting should take place. It is determined by need so apply the rule of, *If it's not needed, don't do it.* So the first question that is asked should be, *Do I need to give this information to Child X or Mrs Y or Mr Z?* This should be followed quickly by the question, *Why?*

Informal reporting can, of course, take place anywhere and at any time, and you should encourage your colleagues to do this. However, in more formal reporting to parents, the time, place and frequency of reports should be planned more carefully.

Think about:
Encourage colleagues to consider:

- *Time:*
  As a general rule, choose a time when there are no other pressures or distractions.

While time seldom allows formal parents' meetings to occur very frequently, the process can be greatly enhanced by regular informal contact.

- *Place:*
  If possible choose a room where comfortable chairs, placed side by side or in a group, can be used. A very different form of interaction takes place when teacher and parents face one another across a desk or table, especially when seated on classroom chairs.

- *Written reports:*
  The time should be chosen to ensure that sufficient evidence is available for making judgments, producing the reports in an appropriate form and giving the recipients time to reflect and respond.

How should reporting be done?

For the reporting of progress and any assessment results to be effective, it should take place in a way which is meaningful for those who are receiving the information. Reporting often depends on the methods used to record the progress and so, as coordinator, you will need to link reporting in science to the school's policy on assessment and record-keeping in science. Since the basis on which assessments are made and justifications for judgments will need to be explored, effective record-keeping and appropriate pieces of evidence should be available for discussion.

Think about:
Are your colleagues collecting information and evidence in a variety of forms for use when reporting?
Think about:
- children's work books;
- work displayed;
- records of achievement;
- portfolios of children's work over time;
- teacher's records;
- other assessment documents.

Both oral and written reporting are important. In both cases, the quantity and nature of information and the words used must be carefully selected.

Does your reporting system take into account issues of format, quantity and nature of information?
Think about:
- the quantity of information presented;
- the focus of the information;
- the need for clear, jargon-free language;
- the context in which the information is set.

Displays for open days and parents evenings can support the sharing of meanings and ensure that there is a clear understanding of what the process of education in science is about. As coordinator, you should think about displays which can be used to support this process.

Summing up

In this chapter, we have discussed your role as science coordinator in connection with monitoring and evaluating children's learning in science across the whole school. We have looked in particular at the relationship between assessment, record-keeping and reporting procedures in relation to this role. Some difficulties you might anticipate and plan for are:

- evaluation of learning in science will need to be considered within a broader school policy on assessment, record-keeping and reporting;
- gaining access to information will require cooperation from your colleagues and so preliminary discussions about purposes and methods will be necessary;
- guidelines on practices may be needed to interpret general policy within the specific context of science.

In the last section, we will look in detail at your role, as coordinator, in managing resources for science, and provide information which might be of use to you as sources of ideas, information and materials.

Chapter 14 Managing resources

Introduction

The management of resources is likely to be an important and potentially time-consuming part of your role as a coordinator. Effective resource provision and management is a crucial aspect of planning for learning at both the school and the classroom level. Resourcing is a whole-school issue but, as the coordinator, you will need to monitor and evaluate the organisation and use of science resources.

In the *Handbook for the Inspection of Schools* (OFSTED, 1993), inspectors will evaluate the learning resources in terms of how they influence standards and learning in relation to their:
- availability;
- accessibility;
- quality; and,
- efficient use.

While these criteria apply generally, you will need to consider them in the context of science.

As you think about each of these, think about how you will provide evidence for inspectors in terms of:
- the variety of learning resources available in the school;
- your budget for resourcing science;
- out-of-school resources and their use.

Suggestion

In relation to your school, think about:
- what resources are available in the school?
- where is equipment currently stored?
- how is it stored?
- how are resources used and by whom?
- what other information do you need?

Variety of learning resources available

When we think about managing resources, we tend to think about the physical equipment children use during practical science activities. But resources are wider than this and their management is more than storage and issue. As science involves exploring that world, the whole biophysical environment is a resource for learning and a science coordinator will need to think about this aspect, too.

You will need to think about appropriate ways to collect information about resources and their use. This could be done by circulating a questionnaire to staff. Alternatively, you may wish to run a session at a staff meeting on resourcing science, and this would then allow you to explore some of the more general issues about resources.

We will begin with resources commonly available in the classroom, the school and the immediate environment. The management of these resources effectively to encourage good science teaching involves a number of basic considerations. First, as the coordinator you must think about the management of space as a resource. Second, the availability of the materials and equipment for use within this space will have to be considered. Third, there is the matter of health and safety related to resource use. Finally, more diverse resources have to be considered.

Space as a resource

Physical space tends not to be seen as a resource and yet it is just as important as the more tangible materials and equipment. You should think about the space available in classrooms and advise colleagues on different ways of using it to good effect. Too often, primary classrooms seem to have too little space. Sometimes, however, the lack of space is more a lack of awareness of what is possible with what exists. Four basic principles apply to the use of classroom space for primary science work. Classroom space should be organised to:

- allow children personal space to work individually, without being cramped and without disturbance;
- allow children to work individually, in pairs or small groups on more space-demanding activities such as practical science investigations;
- allow teachers to store essential resources and children to access them as appropriate;
- allow teachers to move readily from child to child and group to group.

A number of factors influence the effective use space in the classroom: the furniture, how resources are stored and the use of display.

Furniture

The organisation of furniture may seem to have little to do with resourcing primary science but how the chairs and tables are arranged and where the resources are kept can greatly affect the quality of the science experiences provided. In many primary classrooms, convention dictates that children sit in groups, with tables or pairs of desks arranged in clusters for four to six children. While the educational reasons for this arrangement vary, it is likely that most teachers have found this to be one effective use of space. But children sitting in groups to work is not the same as children working as a group. In primary science, we often want children to work as a group on practical investigations. However, the group of six in which they sit for other subjects may not be the most appropriate for science. There are other considerations for rearranging the groups — sex bias, for example, or pair work may be more suitable for the task in hand. In addition, group work is only one of a number of ways children may work in science. There are occasions when the teacher wishes the focus to be on the class as a whole rather than on group activities. At the beginning of a topic, he or she may wish to introduce an idea, or provide some new information through slides or video materials. A piece of equipment may need to be demonstrated or a visitor may be addressing the class. Alternatively, the focus may be on the individual, with a need for quiet reflection and one-to-one discussion. Indeed,

Suggestion

At a staff meeting, encourage the staff to think about the different ways furniture can be arranged in a classroom for different purposes in science. Ask them to think particularly about arrangements best suited to:

- accessing resources
- safety
- introducing new ideas to the whole class
- discussion / reporting back sessions
- practical activity
- recording tasks
- any other?

most teachers know from experience that a few children work better when they are seated on their own and that they actually prefer to work alone on occasions.

Children learn effectively in science through all these approaches and the organisation of the furniture may help or hinder it. Consequently, the arrangement of furniture should allow for these possibilities. No single arrangement suits all kinds of activity for all pupils at all times and it may be that, as the science coordinator, your classroom has to be the showroom for different arrangements at different times.

Storage of resources

In many classrooms, storage space is limited. Shells brought back from holiday, the paper-wasp's old nest found in a garage, rolls of unused wallpaper, clothing catalogues, recycled materials for design and technology that just might be useful — space has to be found for them. Ask teachers about the sorts of things they need to store and get them to classify them into groups. This will help you when it comes to finding the temporary or permanent locations for them. You could ask your colleagues the following questions:

1 Which resources do you use very often, perhaps every day?

Such resources are likely to include those items which are not subject specific, such as scissors and colouring materials. As such they need to easily accessible, perhaps stored on the children's tables or on a side table, and each class needs its own set.

What science resources fall into this category? General resources such as paper and paints, scissors and glue, rulers and plastic containers, come into this group. There is little which is unique to science.

2 Which resources do you use frequently, perhaps once a week?

These resources are likely to include those items which are fairly subject specific, such as protractors or measuring cylinders and textual materials. They need be stored in classroom trolleys or cupboards and be readily accessible as needed.

What science resources fall into this category? Science textual materials would fall into this group. If a commercial scheme is used, workcards could exist in multiple sets so that differentiated tasks or experiences are offered. As far as equipment is concerned, little need be stored permanently in the classroom, although certain items might usefully be available to children at all times when they are involved in practical, investigative science, like magnifiers, storage containers or measuring and timing equipment.

3 *Which resources do you use only occasionally, perhaps once a term?*

Resources which are topic or theme specific, and which perhaps need to be used across the school would fall into this category. Such items would include things which are too costly to buy in multiple quantities or which are used only by one class at a time so more than one (or one set) is unnecessary. These resources could be stored centrally, and given to each class for the half term in which they are to be used.

What science resources fall into this category? Virtually all the science specific materials could do so, and these will be discussed more fully later in this chapter.

4 *Are there resources which you use rarely?*

If there are items which have not been used for a long time, then their usefulness has to be questioned. Are they worth the space? If the answer is no, the solution is to dispose of them. However, in some cases there are interesting or unusual items which can help to make the relevance of science explicit to the children and as such serve as useful scene setters or starting points for discussion.

What science resources fall into this category? These are the idiosyncratic personal items which teachers tend to collect — the paper wasp's nest mentioned earlier, for example, or the collection of light bulbs which ranges from tiny torch bulbs to and enormous 1000 watt stage light bulb. It is useful to you as coordinator to know that such items are available because occasionally they may be of relevance elsewhere, and most teachers are happy to share. Larger items could be stored centrally, in sealed and appropriately labelled boxes.

One thing class teachers need to do is identify which resources will be freely accessible to children, which will only be accessible under supervision and which not at all. Such decisions will need to take into account the age and experience of the children, safety, and factors such as the rarity or fragility of the items concerned. If materials are to be directly accessed by the children, then an appropriate standardised labelling system needs to be agreed by staff and used across the school so that the children become used to it and are able to collect and return resources for themselves. With younger children, colour coding or shadow templates which show where items of equipment are to be placed are helpful, but name labels should also be included on trays or shelves. This helps to make the children more independent and saves time.

Display areas

Children's work in science can become a resource in itself. Displays of their work serve several important purposes.

Good quality displays can:
- motivate children by creating a supportive, encouraging classroom climate for further work;
- give positive feedback to the children and show that their efforts are valued;
- show interested outsiders (other children, teachers, parents and visitors) what has been achieved in science; and,
- show that science is seen as an area of educational experience for children.

Display areas for science should be three-dimensional, including resources, models and activities as well as the more usual two-dimensional pictures, writing and graphs. Displays are more than an opportunity to show examples of children's work; they are also a teaching and learning aid, providing stimuli and ideas, motivating and exciting and sometimes encouraging interaction with the various items on

Suggestion

Think about what your own views are on the use of displays in science:

■ Have a walk around your school and list the opportunities for different kinds of displays in different contexts.

■ How can you encourage your colleagues to use displays in science to advantage?

■ Do you need to produce some guidelines on displays of children's work in science?

■ What about mechanical matters, such as how often should displays be changed?

■ Talk to the art coordinator about displays.

display. A science workstation (see p. 156) will serve these purposes and provide storage space for resources and a place to work.

Schools often have distinctive approaches to display, with rules about double- or triple-mounting and labelling. Nevertheless, displays may become nothing more than wallpaper for the classroom. If a display is to serve an educational function children must look at them and use them. This means they should be at child height, not adult height. Significant aspects of the display should be clearly marked to draw attention to them. Interaction with the display may be encouraged through the use of questions. Children's attention can be drawn to simple activities or an experiment may be offered which cannot be carried out by all the class because of shortage of resources. The children should be encouraged to use the display, and feel they have participated in it.

A final point — displays do not have to be confined to the classroom. You should encourage your colleagues to use corridors or the school hall to show the kinds of science experiences the children have. One class's display can be a teaching resource for the whole school.

Budgets and finances

As the coordinator for science you may well have allocated to you a small budget to spend on resources. Even if you do not have a budget allocated to you on a regular basis, you should be able to approach your headteacher for money for particular purposes to do with resourcing science. The headteacher will need to show that the finances in the school are planned to cover expenditure on all areas of the curriculum for all children. As such, if you show there is a need, then the headteacher will be able to budget to meet that need, although she or he may not be able to do so immediately. This brings us back to the importance of planning in collaboration with the headteacher.

You should also keep your eyes open for alternative sources of funding for science. For example,

- Read carefully through professional journals and magazines. Are there any advertisements for grants to schools for science activities which you could apply for?
- Some businesses and industries make awards to schools for projects in science. Can you design a project for some of your children — perhaps your own class or possibly the whole school — so that you can apply for an award?
- Are there any local companies or manufacturers who may be willing to sponsor science in your school, either with money or with equipment?
- Contact the heads of science in your local secondary schools or the tutor in charge of science at a local higher education institution to ask for first refusal of any equipment and resources which they may no longer want.

Managing science equipment

In the past, primary science teaching has suffered from the 'jam jar' image, specialised equipment being considered unsuitable for primary children. It is true that there is a lot of secondary school science equipment which is inappropriate for primary school children but there is science equipment available which can and should be used. For example, infant children can use pooters to gather minibeasts from hedgerows much more carefully and humanely than using a spoon or paint brush to try to trap the animal in a jar. Junior pupils can use stopwatches for accurate timing and test meters to check whether or not a battery is flat.

One of your tasks as the coordinator will be to list the specialist science resources you already have in the school and what is needed. Purchase of expensive items or items which are only to be of use to one class, may be difficult to justify, especially when school budgets are tight. In these circumstances, you may be able to contact a local secondary school and arrange to borrow the necessary items, or else obtain help from a local teachers' centre, especially where there is a science support team or advisory teacher for science. It is useful if you draw up for staff a list of items not available in school but available from elsewhere on loan. Items of this nature may include a full-size skeleton for doing some work on 'Ourselves', or a collection of fossils. As Burton (1994) points out,

 Restricted funding makes it essential to manage resources for science efficiently. (p. 15)

He identifies four stages for the science coordinator to work through when thinking about resources.

1 List all science resources available in the school and identify strengths and weaknesses in resourcing.
2 Design and if possible allocate a set of basic equipment for each class, including assorted recyclable and other materials.
3 Through staff discussion, identify a central storage area for the remainder of the resources and also how resource needs can be matched to patterns of teaching.
4 Implement the storage and retrieval system.

As the coordinator, you will then need to think about the collecting and buying of extra materials. This will involve decisions about how to spend the money allocated for purchase of science resources for the school. Some coordinators deal with this by sharing the money between teachers so they may order things to suit their topics. This needs to be carefully monitored if unnecessary duplication is to be avoided. It also means that more expensive items can rarely be purchased. It is usually better to do an audit of what is already available, match these items to the topics taught and the timing of those topics in the science programme, and determine what is needed. In this way, over time, stock can be built up. It allows the coordinator to begin a stock book, monitor what there is, replace consumables and broken items, and add to the stock when money is available. It also allows for more efficient use of resources across classes and accommodates different ways of working.

An approach of this kind will require some central storage and monitoring of resources. There are various options, with advantages and disadvantages for each. These are summarised in Figure 14.1 (p. 184). The options should be discussed with staff and the pros and cons considered. Ideally, the staff

FIG 14.1
Options for storing resources

Possible Systems	Advantages	Disadvantages
Central Store: all resources kept together; sorted by resource, e.g. all measuring instruments together; perhaps shelved alphabetically	■ no duplication of equipment needed ■ storage space is minimised ■ easily accessible to teachers and pupils ■ easy for a new teacher to use ■ spontaneous science possible	■ difficult for children to use without supervision ■ takes time for teachers to collect/return the resources properly ■ difficult for the science coordinator to check the resources in and out ■ needs a very organised school science programme
Box Storage: using uniform size boxes, stored in a central location; each box to contain all resources needed for a single unit of work; labelled appropriately, e.g. 'Air', 'Electricity', 'Seeds'	■ suitable for use with workcards and sheets ■ easy for children and teachers to collect and return ■ once set up, easy to manage ■ very organised, so it supports teachers who lack confidence ■ suits any type of class room organisation	■ time consuming to set up initially ■ duplicate resources are needed which costs more ■ boxes must be checked on return ■ large or expensive items will still need to be stored separately ■ flexibility / spontaneity are greatly reduced
Topic Storage: all resources needed for science activities within a particular topic kept together, either in a central store or in the classroom of the teacher who does that topic	■ reduces teachers' preparation prior to the lesson ■ can be kept for a long period of time in one classroom ■ teachers can add things to personalise the box	■ large quantities of resources needed, so can be very costly ■ duplication of resources necessary ■ requires a lot of storage space ■ inhibits spontaneous science activity ■ some teachers may hoard resources

as a whole should decide on the system they want, since they are going to have to work with it.

Whatever system is chosen, you will be the one to manage it and you need to consider matters like:

■ *Where will the resources be stored when not in use?*
   e.g. in a central store, in the coordinator's classroom, shared across all classrooms;
■ *Who will have access?*
   e.g. the coordinator only, other teachers, KS2 children, all children;
■ *When will resources be accessible?*
   e.g. during lessons, at lunchtime, afternoons only, one afternoon a week;
■ *Will some items need to be kept secure?*
   e.g. sharp objects, heavy items, expensive items;
■ *How will they be stored?*
   e.g. in crates or boxes, on open shelves, on silhouette shelves, in labelled topic packs;
■ *how will they be collected and returned?*
   e.g. by the coordinator only, by teachers, by children.

One of the problems for any science coordinator of central resource management is checking resources back in after use, and ensuring that nothing is missing, damaged or broken, and that consumables are replaced. If resources are boxed or crated according to topics this is easier to do. A duplicated sheet in a plastic wallet can list all the items in the crate, with quantities, when the resources are handed over to the teacher who intends to use them. At the end of the topic, the class teacher takes responsibility for checking the contents before returning them to you and indicating if there is anything missing or broken. It is much easier to run down checklists like this than to monitor individual items. There will still be a need to monitor the diverse small items, like magnifiers, which are used across topics. It is better to give each teacher his or her own class set of such resources. If this is not possible, then a card system can be operated for checking such items in and out. For example, the school's supply of twenty hand lens may be stored in a labelled box with a card which states how many magnifiers there are. The teacher who borrows them signs and dates the card and leaves it in an 'out' tray. The card is then kept by you until the magnifiers are returned. If someone else needs them, their location is known. When they are returned, the coordinator can check them, sign off the card and return them to the cupboard. A borrowing book can work in a similar way. Such a system also allows the coordinator to check equipment for safety and initiate repairs and replacements. The cost of repairs needs to be built into the budget.

Safety and resources

Safety in science has already been identified as a major concern for science coordinators. With safety matters, you must always be guided by your own school and local education authority regulations. Generally, safety is the responsibility of your employer, that is either the education authority or governing body. Most follow advice provided by COSHH: *Guidance for Schools* (HMSO, 1989), and the Code of Practice which accompanies the Management of Health and Safety at Work Regulations of 1992, although both of these really apply to secondary schools and workplaces. For safety in primary school science, one of your best sources of advice and information is *Be Safe! Some aspects of safety in science and technology for key stages 1 and 2* (ASE, 1990). This has generally been adopted by most education authorities to guide their safety policy and risk assessment procedures, and is likely to be used by inspectors as their guide on what to look for during inspections.

As the coordinator, you need to ensure that:
- The science policy statement, schemes of work and planning at the classroom level all contain evidence of safety awareness.
- All staff are aware, at the informal level, of the need for safe practice in science and that there is a consistency in action across the school by children as well as teachers.
- That resources are managed in a safe way, reflecting not only tidy and safe storage but also understanding of recommendations about the suitability of particular resources for use in primary science.

Probably one of the best things you can do, as the science coordinator, is produce an A4 sheet summarising for colleagues the basic principles of safe practice in science, which should be accessible at all times in their planning files or some other suitable place. This could include a very simple audit sheet, which you or your colleagues could use to check for safe practice. Some basic things you may need to think about are:

Regular Safety Audits: As the coordinator, you should carry out general audits of equipment and materials for safety. This could be part of your annual review of provision. At a more specific level, encourage colleagues to audit provision, in the sense of running through the audit checklist when they do their detailed half-termly planning.

Resources that are Being Used: Most equipment and resources for primary science are safe both to use and to store. However, some items may need particular handling and supervision.

What is the school/LEA policy on the use of:
- hot water — how hot? how heated?
- heat sources — night-light candles? other candles? picnic stoves? heating rings? cookers?
- containers — plastic? glass?
- chemicals — what can be used? kitchen chemistry?
- batteries — ordinary batteries? re-chargeable batteries? power packs?
- food stuffs — fresh? mouldy? cooking? eating?
- ourselves and other animals — what is and is not safe to do and use?

Supervision of Activities in Classrooms: Most activities will not need close supervision, but some will. A teacher cannot 'closely supervise' 30+ children at once. Does planning allow for this? Can other adults be used for supervision purposes? Are there alternative activities instead?

Be Safe! covers all of these matters and many more, and as a coordinator you should try to get hold of a copy for your own reference. A final point you need to think about is how safety in science relates to the school's more general accident and safety policy. In the unlikely event of an accident occurring during a science lesson or activity, do you and your colleagues know what to do?

Further support is available for you from the Association for Science Education's (ASE) Safeguards in Science Committee, which will provide advice on health and safety matters to ASE members. The ASE has more recently produced an INSET pack for coordinators to use on training days with colleagues, *Safety in Science for Primary Schools: An INSET Pack* (ASE, 1994). Another source of help and advice on safety in science is CLEAPSS — the Consortium of Local Education Authorities for the provision of Science Services. Over 95 per cent of education authorities in England, Wales and Northern Ireland are members of CLEAPSS, which as well as providing information and support generally, run a helpline for schools.

Summing up

In this chapter we have discussed some of the things you will need to think about when managing the science resources in your school. In particular, you need to think about safety. Some difficulties you might anticipate and plan for include:
- security for expensive or fragile items;
- the non-return of resources;
- the non-reporting of damage to resources;
- safety and the management and use of resources.

Some solutions have been suggested which are feasible in most primary school situations.

| Chapter 15 | Information and resources for science coordinators |

Introduction

We said in Chapter 1 that science coordinators should not see themselves as working alone and without support. There are various materials and resources that can help you in your role. What follows in this chapter is a summary of those most readily available but, inevitably, the list cannot be complete. Commercially produced schemes, for example, have not been included although we recognise that some provide very good support materials which you can use to help teachers turn ideas into reality. They also give structure to planning and assessment.

In this section, we will list some details of some support materials we feel you should be aware of as the science coordinator. This list includes:
■ suggestions for background reading for coordinators;
■ sources for ideas for INSET and staff development sessions;
■ associations which provide support for teaching primary science;
■ journals published by these associations;
■ some suppliers' addresses;
■ sources of industry/enterprise links; and,
■ interactive science and technology centres.

As the coordinator, you may also come across free resources which might help you and your colleagues. For example,

Suggestion

- You should write to as many publishers, suppliers and other contacts as possible, asking to be placed on their mailing lists for catalogues and other information.
- Ask your headteacher for a small amount of money so that you can buy some storage boxes from an office suppliers for cataloguing the information in an appropriate way.
- Go through your local telephone directory and find out where there are manufacturers who may be willing to give you free or cheap materials which will be of use in science.
- Send a letter home to parents, listing what sorts of things might be useful in teaching science and asking them whether or not they have any useful contacts.

many of the large superstores produce leaflets for customers which describe how they are being environmentally friendly. Some building societies produce advice leaflets on buildings and structures. Electricity and gas board shops often have leaflets on energy efficiency in the home. Post offices sometimes have posters and materials on aspects of communication. Ask for copies for yourself and your colleagues, or even class-size sets. You will usually find the business or store very helpful.

Background reading

You should have a small stock of books on your own bookshelf which support you with background knowledge and information about science and science education. For example,

■ Bradley, L.S. (1996) *Children Learning Science*, Oxford: Nash Pollock Publishing.
(Provides a very good overview of how young children learn in science, both informally and formally; well illustrated with classroom examples, it relates children's learning to matters of planning, organising and assessing science in primary classrooms.)

■ Goldsworthy, A. and Feasey, R. (1994) *Making Sense of Primary Science Investigations*, Hatfield: ASE.
(Aims to answer questions about the process of scientific investigation across KS 1 and 2 in a clear and straightforward way; deals with matters related to designing complete investigations, handling variables, and progression in investigative skills.)

■ Newton, L.D. and Newton, D.P. (1995) *A Question of Science: Science Information for Primary Teachers*, INPUTS Series, London: Watts Books.
(Covers the basic science knowledge base which all primary teachers need in order to meet the National Curriculum requirements for science, and puts this into a context for classroom practice.)

■ Sherrington, R. (ed.) (1993) *The ASE Primary Science Teacher's Handbook*, Hemel Hempstead: Simon and Schuster Education.
(Presents discussions on issues related to the teaching of science and science education pedagogy; for example, aims and purposes, how children learn in science, strategies and approaches, assessment and science for all.)

INSET/staff development ideas

You do not have to re-invent the wheel! There are a number of good resource packs which contain ideas for running staff development sessions. For example,

■ ASE (1994) *Safety in Science for Primary Schools: An INSET Pack*, Hatfield: ASE.
(Designed for coordinators to use when running safety-focused staff development sessions in their schools; contains a safety checklist, advice on developing a safety policy, a range of activities and photocopiable materials.)

■ Clayden, E. and Peacock, A. (1994) *Science for Curriculum Leaders*, London: Routledge.
(A sourcebook of INSET ideas, organised into units, each of which focuses on an issue in science education which may be causing concern for primary teachers.)

■ Harlen, W., Macro, C., Schilling, M., Malvern, D. and Reed, K. (1990) *Progress in Primary Science*, London: Routledge.
(Designed to provide opportunities to explore different aspects of teaching and learning in primary science; module structure, with each module in two parts, notes for the coordinator or course leader, and activities and information for the participants.)

Associations

While you do not have to be a member of a science group or association, you will find that it is a good way to keep informed and share ideas.

Association for Science Education (ASE)

The ASE has a long history of support for science teaching, initially in secondary schools but now in primary schools as well. They publish the *School Science Review* three times a year to share ideas about the teaching of school science. Although aimed at secondary school teaching, it always had an 'elementary science' section. Anticipating the National Curriculum, the ASE expanded into primary school science teaching in 1986, publishing the *Primary Science Review.* This has been a major source of ideas and information for primary teachers since then. The ASE produces a range of books and guidance materials for teachers, which are advertised in *PSR* and can be purchased at a 10 per cent discount by members. The association also organises local and national meetings, and runs an advice and support system. There are different categories of membership; teachers can subscribe as individuals or schools can take out a group subscription.

Contact:

Membership: The Membership Manager
Freepost
The Association for Science Education
College Lane
Hatfield
Herts. AL10 9BR
Telephone: 01707–267411

British Association for the Advancement of Science (BAAS)

The British Association aims to support and promote science at all levels. It holds an annual festival of science, open to schools, other institutions and the general public, and produces *SCAN*, a science awareness newsletter. At the primary school level, the BA supports the BAYS club scheme (British Association for Young Scientists) for 8- to 18-year-olds, organising science challenges and awarding bronze, silver and gold level certificates. The BA also holds a national database of speakers on science and technology, called Talking Science Plus.

Contact:

Membership: The British Association for the Advancement
of Science
Fortress House
23, Savile Row
London W1X 1AB
Telephone: 0171–494–3326

Earth Science Teachers' Association (ESTA)

ESTA publishes journals for teachers at both primary and secondary school levels, containing ideas and information related particularly to aspects of geology; it also organises in-service meetings and conferences (see *Teaching Primary Earth Science*, p. 196). There are special rates for members buying rock and mineral samples, books, maps and postcards.

Contact:

Membership: Mrs K. York
ESTA Primary Committee
346, Middlewood Road North
Oughtibridge
Sheffield S30 3HF

Consortium of Local Education Authorities for the Provision of Science Services (CLEAPSS)

About 95 per cent of all local education authorities in England, Wales and Northern Ireland are members of CLEAPSS, and it is also possible for schools and colleges to join independently. Its aim is to support the teaching of practical science and technology through a range of publications and also the provision of in-service courses. It is particularly helpful with advice on resources and equipment and health and safety issues. Check whether or not your own LEA is a member, and if so make sure you are on the mailing list for the publications and information.

Contact:

Information: CLEAPSS School Science Service
Brunel University
Uxbridge
UB8 3PH
Helpline: 01895–251496
Fax: 01895–814372

Journals and professional magazines

There are a number of journals and professional magazines that you should try to look at on a regular basis, both for ideas and to keep yourself informed. Most should be available through your local university library.

Education in Chemistry (EiC)

This is a professional journal for teachers, published by the Institute of Chemistry four times a year. It is aimed at secondary science teachers, but sometimes contains information useful to the primary science coordinator.

International Journal for Science Education (IJSE)

This is a leading journal which brings together the latest research in science education from around the world, published four times a year. Although not of general use for the non-specialist primary science teacher, it will be of interest to science coordinators who wish to go beyond their immediate role and keep up with developments in science education for their own benefit.

Journal of Biological Education (JBE)

This is a professional journal for teachers, published by the Institute of Biology four times a year. As with *EiC*, it is aimed at secondary science teachers, but sometimes contains information useful to the primary science coordinator.

Physics Education (PE)

This is a professional journal for teachers, published by the Institute of Physics four times a year. Again, as with *EiC* and *JBE*, it is aimed at secondary science teachers, but sometimes contains information useful to the primary science coordinator.

Primary Science Review (PSR)

First issued in Summer 1986, *PSR* is now published five times a year by the ASE, and is the primary science journal for the association. It includes articles and information on science, D&T and IT, as well as having a research round-up section, book reviews and information about conferences and meetings. For details of the address and membership, see under ASE (p. 192).

Questions of Maths and Science (QMS)

Originally *Questions: Exploring Science and Technology 3–13* and first published in October 1988, this professional publication for teachers combined in 1996 with its mathematics equivalent, *Strategies*, to form the new *Questions of Maths and Science* (*QMS*). Published nine times a year, it provides articles and information for teachers covering subject knowledge and application, new books and resources, support organisations, meetings and conferences. It also includes pull-out teaching packs, usually topic focused, containing ideas and materials for immediate use in the classroom. In Autumn 1997, **QMS** became **Primary Maths and Science**.

Contact:

Order from:	Questions Publishing Company
	27, Frederick Street
	Birmingham
	B1 3HH
Contact:	Fran Stevens
Telephone:	0121–212–0919
Fax:	0121–212–0959

Teaching Primary Earth Science (TPES)

This is a journal for primary teachers, produced by the Earth Science Teachers' Association four times a year. It provides ideas, activities and information on Earth Science topics based on NC Science and Geography; it also provides details of in-service conferences and materials and resources useful for teaching in the primary school. For details of the address and membership, see under ESTA (p. 193).

The Young Detectives Magazine

This is a new magazine produced by BNFL in summer 1996. It contains news, ideas and resources for Primary Science and Technology, and is issued free three times a year.

Contact:

Contact:	*The Young Detectives Magazine*
	Resources for Learning
	19, Park Drive
	Bradford
	West Yorkshire
	BD9 4DS
Telephone:	01274–544155

Some suppliers

The list of possible suppliers of science resources and equipment is enormous, and some schools are restricted by their LEA's to purchasing from particular ones. However, if you do have a choice it is worth shopping around because prices can vary tremendously. Some you might look at include the following.

Heron Educational Ltd

Heron provide a range of resources from furniture and workstations to tools and equipment. They publish different catalogues for Primary Science, Primary Technology and Early Years.

Contact:

Heron Educational Ltd
Carrwood House
Carrwood Road
Chesterfield S41 9QB
Telephone: 0800–373249 (free)

Insect Lore

This firm provides resources related to studying the natural world (CD-roms, books, videos, posters, kits, puppets, and other materials). A catalogue is available.

Contact:

Insect Lore (Europe)
Suite 6, Linford Forum
Linford Wood
Milton Keynes MK14 6LY
Telephone: 01908–200794
Fax: 01908–200793

NES Arnold educational supplier

Although a general educational supplier, NES Arnold offer a range of resources to support primary science teaching. As well as the large general catalogue, a primary science catalogue is available.

Contact:

NES Arnold Ltd
Ludlow Hill Road
West Bridgford
Nottingham NG2 6HD
Telephone: 0115–945–2200

NIAS — Northamptonshire Inspection and Advisory Service

This is a science centre that provides a range of resources to schools, both kits and textual materials, to support the teaching of primary science in schools. Produced by their advisory teams for their own schools, the materials are closely tied to the needs of schools and have often been prepared in consultation with school staff. The resources are often advertised in the *Primary Science Review*.

Contact:

NIAS
The Science Centre
Spencer Centre
Lewis Road
Northants NN5 7BJ

Pictorial Charts Educational Trust (PCET)

PCET provides wallcharts and illustrated materials to support the teaching of science; extensive range and high quality.

Contact:

PCET
27 Kirchen Road
London W13 0UD
Telephone: 0181–5679206

Small-life Supplies

This firm supplies a range of living things for the classroom that are both easy to keep and safe to use. They also supply cages, books, tapes, posters and foodstuff. An illustrated talk service is also available. A catalogue is available on request.

Contact:

Small-Life Supplies
Normanton Lane Industrial Estate
Bottesford
Notts NG13 0EL
Telephone: 01949–842446
Fax: 01949–843036

Technology Teaching Systems (TTS)

Despite its misleading name, TTS provides a full range of resources for teaching primary science. A catalogue is available giving full details.

Contact:

TTS
Unit 4, Holmewood Fields Business Park
Park Road
Holmewood
Chesterfield S42 5UY

Ways and means

This is a small firm specialising in science and D&T resources for primary schools. A catalogue is available on request.

Contact:

Ways and Means (Equipment Suppliers)
3, Mazine Terrace
Haswell
Co. Durham DH6 2EF
Telephone: 0191–526–6908

Industry, enterprise and other links

The DFE published a booklet in 1993 called *Building Effective School–Business Links.* This details ways in which schools can enhance their links with industry and business, and maximise the value of such links.

British Kidney Patient Association

A teaching resources pack is available which includes a ten-minute video, classroom poster, teacher's guide and photocopiable sheets for use in the classroom and at home. It is aimed a 9–14-year-olds. The pack is free but a small charge is made to cover package and postage.

Contact:

The British Kidney Patient Association
Bordon
Hampshire GU35 9JZ
Telephone: 01420–472021

British Nuclear Fuels Ltd (BNFL)

BNFL produce video materials, booklets and posters, resource
packs and other resources to support school science teaching
at the primary as well as secondary school levels. Visits to
power stations and energy centres can also be arranged with
the education officers. A free catalogue is available.

Contact:

BNFL
Community Affairs
Risley
Warrington
Cheshire WA3 9AS
Telephone: 01925–832826

The Chemical Industry Education Centre (CIEC)

The CIEC at the University of York works with teachers and
industrialists to write teaching materials which make science
and technology experiences explicitly relevant to primary
and secondary pupils. For primary school use, over twenty
theme-related units are available; for example, *Tidy and Sort*
(for 5–7-year-olds) and *Plastics Playtime* (for 8–10-year-olds).
Each unit contains teacher's notes, background information
and photocopiable activity sheets. A catalogue is available
on request.

Contact:

CIEC
Department of Chemistry
University of York
York YO1 5DD
Telephone: 01904–432523

Institution of Electrical Engineers

This institute produces a range of resources to support school science. For primary schools, recent resources (books, topic packs and video materials) focus on supporting the teaching of electricity, energy and control.

Contact:

> The Institution of Electrical Engineers
> Michael Faraday House
> Six Hills Way
> Stevenage
> Herts SG1 2AY
>
> *Telephone:* 01438–313311

Royal Society for the Protection of Birds (RSPB)

The RSPB have a network of education officers around the country who will visit schools and give talks on topics related to birds. Teaching resource materials are also available and schools as well as individuals can apply for membership.

Contact:

> The RSPB Education Office
> The Lodge
> Sandy
> Beds SG19 2DL

The School Curriculum Industry Partnership (SCIP)

SCIP is an organisation which aims to promote partnership between education and industry and support the education of pupils between the ages of 5 and 19 years.

Contact:

> Centre for Education and Industry
> University of Warwick
> Coventry CV4 7AL
>
> *Telephone:* 01203–524372

Standing Conference on Schools' Science and Technology (SCSST)

This is the organisation which runs the SATROs (the Science and Technology Regional Organisation) partnerships between education, business and industry, from which very useful resource materials can be purchased; for example, electrical components such as bulbs and wires. Each centre usually produces its own list of supplies available to schools. SCSST also organises the CREST Awards for creativity in science and technology (with the British Association for the Advancement of Science).

Contact:

SCSST
1, Giltspur Street
London EC1A 9DD
Telephone: 0171–294–2468

Understanding British Industry (UBI)

The UBI provides information on businesses and organisations who offer information, support and links with schools. Teacher placement schemes are also included.

Contact:

The UBI
101, Lakesmere Close
Kidlington Business Centre
Kidlington
Oxon OX5 1LG
Telephone: 01865–374389

Interactive Science and Technology Centres (ISTCs)

ISTCs are fashionable, being one way to take science and technology to the wider public and aimed at changing people's perceptions of and attitudes towards science and technology. Their focus is a hands-on approach, which enables sensory interaction, which interests and motivates all involved. As with museums, a preliminary visit by the science coordinator is advisable to assess how it might be used, make contacts and see what kind of support is available during visits. There are ISTCs spread nationally in most of our large cities, and some of the more well known are listed here:

Discovery Dome
    c/o Science Projects
    Turnham Green
    Terrace Mews
    London W1 1QU

Glasgow Dome of Discovery
    South Rotunda
    100 Govan Road
    Glasgow G51 1JS

Light on Science
    Birmingham Museum of
      Science and Industry
    Newhall Street
    Birmingham B3 1RX

Technology Testbed
    National Museums and
      Galleries on Merseyside
    Large Objects Collection
    Princes Dock
    Pier Head
    Liverpool L3 0AA

The Exploratory
    The Old Station
    Temple Meads
    Bristol BS8 1QU

Launch Pad
    Science Museum
    Exhibition Road
    London SW7 2DD

Science Factory
    Newcastle Museum of
      Science and Engineering
    Blandford Street
    Newcastle upon Tyne
    NE1 4JA

Xperiment!
    Greater Manchester
      Museum of Science and
      Industry
    Castlefield
    Manchester M3 4JP

Further help with IT

If you find yourself working in a school where there is no-one with responsibility for IT, and your own expertise in this area is not great, then a useful starting point for thinking about IT in science would be Mike Harrison's chapter 'Getting IT Together in Key Stage 2', in his book for coordinators at Key Stage 2 (Harrison, 1995). There are also two special issues of *Primary Science Review* (December

1991 and December 1995) which focus exclusively on the use of IT in science.

Help with IT can also be obtained from a number of sources. Try your local education authority advisory service. They should be able to put you in touch with someone. Organisations such as the ASE and NCET can also help by providing publications and teaching materials. ASE run regional meetings and conferences, often including IT in their programme. NCET produces leaflets and information packages on hardware and software. It has also commissioned a series of television programmes on the use of IT in schools.

Contact:

> The Science Information Officer
> NCET
> Milburn Hill Road
> Science Park
> Coventry CV4 7JJ
> *Telephone:*   01203–416994 (enquiry service)

Fifty-three Local Education Authorities also have SEMERC centres — computer centres offering training, advice and support in all areas of computer use in school. Many of the centres also supply SEMERC software to their local schools, often at a discount. Further information and a catalogue is available.

Contact:

> SEMERC
> 1, Broadbent Road
> Watersheddings
> Oldham OL1 4LB
> *Telephone:*   0161–627–4469

References

Association for Science Education (ASE) (1986) 'Primary Science: ASE policy', *Primary Science Review*, **1**, September, p. 18.

Association for Science Education (ASE) (1990) *Be Safe! Some Aspects of Safety in School Science and Technology for Key Stages 1 and 2* (2nd edition), Hatfield: ASE.

Association for Science Education (ASE) (1991) 'Primary science review — special on information technology', *Primary Science Review*, **20**, December.

Association for Science Education (ASE) (1994) *Safety in Science for Primary Schools*, Hatfield: ASE.

Association for Science Education (ASE) (1995) 'Primary science review — special on information technology and science', *Primary Science Review*, **40**, December.

Bell, D. (1992) 'Co-ordinating science in primary schools: A role model?', in Newton, L.D. *Primary Science: The Challenge of the 1990s*, Clevedon: Multiligual Matters, pp. 93–109.

Bradley, L.S. (1996) *Children Learning Science*, Oxford: Nash Pollock Publishing.

Burton, N. (1994) 'Organising science resources', *Primary Science Review*, **31**, February, pp. 15–16.

Cavalcante, P.S., Newton, L.D. and Newton, D.P. (1996) 'Primary science teaching — facts or procedures? Do different teaching approaches influence children's learning?', Paper presented at the Annual Conference of the British Educational Research Association, Lancaster, September 1996.

CLAYDEN, E. and PEACOCK, A. (1994) *Science for Curriculum Leaders*, London: Routledge.

COLLINGS, J. (1994) 'The significance of AT1', *Primary Science Review*, **34**, October, pp. 23–24.

DEPARTMENT FOR EDUCATION (DfE) (1992) *Guidance on Audits of Teaching Staff*, London: HMSO.

DEPARTMENT FOR EDUCATION (DfE) (1995) *Science in the National Curriculum*, London: HMSO.

DEPARTMENT OF EDUCATION AND SCIENCE (DES) (1978) *Primary Education in England: A Survey by Her Majesty's Inspectors of Schools*, London: HMSO.

DEPARTMENT OF EDUCATION AND SCIENCE (DES) (1984) *Science in the Primary School*, London: HMSO.

DEPARTMENT OF EDUCATION AND SCIENCE (DES) (1985) *Science 5–16: A Statement of Policy*, London: HMSO.

DEPARTMENT OF EDUCATION AND SCIENCE (DES) (1988) *National Curriculum: First Report of the Task Group on Assessment and Testing*, London: HMSO.

DEPARTMENT OF EDUCATION AND SCIENCE (DES) (1989) *The Teaching and Learning of Science*, (HMI Aspects of Primary Education Series), London: HMSO.

DEPARTMENT OF EDUCATION AND SCIENCE (DES) (1990) *Circular 3/90: National Curriculum Orders*, London: HMSO.

EDMONDS, J. and MANFORD, L. (1996) 'A process of science policy development', *Primary Science Review*, **41**, February, pp. 8–10.

HAIGH, G. (1996) 'Dreams of empire', *Times Educational Supplement* (TES School Management Update), 19 January, p. 6.

HARLEN, W. (1983) *Guides to Assessment in Education: Science*, London: Macmillan.

HARLEN, W. (1991) 'Research roundup', *Primary Science Review*, **16**, February, p. 18.

HARLEN, W. (1992) *The Teaching of Science*, London: David Fulton Publishing Limited.

HARLEN, W., MACRO, C., SCHILLING, M., MALVERN, D. and REED, K. (1990) *Progress in Primary Science*, London: Routledge.

HARRIS, S. (1996) *Science in Primary Schools*, Slough: NFER.

HARRISON, M. (ed.) (1995) *Developing a Leadership Role in Key Stage 2 Curriculum*, London: Falmer Press.

HARRISON, M. (1996) 'Who's watching who?' *Times Educational Supplement* (TES School Management Update), 19 January, p. 7.

HARRISON, M. and CROSS, A (1994) 'Successful curriculum change through co-ordination', in HARRISON, M. (ed.) *Beyond the Core Curriculum*, Plymouth: Northcote House, Chapter 2.

HATANO, G. and INAGAKI, K. (1992) 'Desituating cognition through the construction of conceptual knowledge', in LIGHT, P. and BUTTERWORTH, G. (eds) *Content and Cognition: Ways of Learning and Knowing*, London: Harvester-Wheatsheaf, pp. 115–33.

HAWKEY, R. (1995) 'Primary children's expectations of secondary school science', *Primary Science Review*, **39**, October, pp. 16–17.

HER MAJESTY'S INSPECTORATE (1991) *Science: Key Stages 1 and 3. A Report by HMI on the First Year, 1989–1990*, London: HMSO.

HER MAJESTY'S INSPECTORATE (1993) *Science in Key Stage 1, 2 and 3: Third Year, 1991–92*, London: HMSO.

HER MAJESTY'S STATIONERY OFFICE (1989) *Control of Substances Hazardous to Health (COSHH): Guidance for Schools*, London: HMSO.

HOLROYD, C. and HARLEN, W. (1995) 'Teachers' understanding of science: A cause for concern', *Primary Science Review*, **39**, October, pp. 23–25.

JARMAN, R. (1984) *Primary Science/Secondary Science: Some Issues at the Interface*, London: Secondary Science Curriculum Review.

MCGRATH, C. (1995) 'Where have the attainment targets gone?', *Primary Science Review*, **38**, June, p. 3.

MORRISON, K. (1985) 'Tensions in subject–specialist teaching in the primary school', *Curriculum*, **6**, 3, pp. 24–29.

NATIONAL CURRICULUM COUNCIL (NCC) (1989) *Non-Statutory Guidance for Science in the National Curriculum*, York: NCC.

NATIONAL CURRICULUM COUNCIL (NCC) (1990) *Curriculum Guidance 3: The Whole Curriculum*, York: NCC.

NATIONAL CURRICULUM COUNCIL (NCC) (1993) *Teaching Science at Key Stages 1 and 2*, York: NCC.

NELLIST, J. (1986) 'Primary futures', *Primary Science Review*, **1**, Summer, pp. 2–3.

NEWTON, D.P. (1990) 'Choosing Software — A Software Evaluation Schedule', *Information Technology and Learning*, December, pp. 83–86.

NEWTON, D.P. (1992) 'Children doing science: Observation, investigation and the National Curriculum for England and Wales', in NEWTON, L.D. (ed.) *Primary Science: The Challenge of the 1990s*, Clevedon: Multilingual Matters, pp. 8–19.

NEWTON, D.P. and NEWTON, L.D. (1997) 'Has the National Curriculum changed children's minds about scientists?', *British Journal of Curriculum and Assessment*, **7**, 2, pp. 24–26.

NEWTON, L.D. (1987) 'Co-ordinating science in a small primary school', *Primary Science Review*, **4**, Summer, pp. 14–15.

NEWTON, L.D. (ed.) (1992) *Primary Science: The Challenge of the 1990s*, Clevedon: Multilingual Matters.

NEWTON, L.D. (1996) 'Teachers' questioning in primary school science: Developing children's causal understanding through a mental model approach', Unpublished PhD thesis: University of Newcastle upon Tyne.

NEWTON, L.D. and NEWTON, D.P. (1993) 'Investigation in National Curriculum science: Some definitions', *Primary Science Review*, **30**, December, pp. 15–17.

NEWTON, L.D. and NEWTON, D.P. (1995) *A Question of Science*, London: Watts Books.

OFFICE FOR STANDARDS IN EDUCATION (1993) *Science: Key Stages 1, 2, 3 and 4; Fourth Year, 1992–93*, London: HMSO/OFSTED.

OFFICE FOR STANDARDS IN EDUCATION (1994a) *Primary Matters: A Discussion on Teaching and Learning in Primary Schools*, London: HMSO/OFSTED.

OFFICE FOR STANDARDS IN EDUCATION (1994b) *Science and Mathematics in Schools: A Review*, London: HMSO/OFSTED.

OVENS, P. (1994) 'Class size and research styles', *Primary Science Review*, **35**, December, pp. 2–3.

PREEDY, P. and TAYLOR, H. (1991) 'Classroom–based INSET', *Primary Science Review*, **16**, February, pp. 4–5.

QUALTER, A. (1996) *Differentiated Primary Science*, Buckingham: Open University Press.

RUSSELL, T., BELL, D., MCGUIGAN, L., QUALTER, A., QUINN, J. and SCHILLING, M. (1992) 'Teachers' conceptual understanding in science: Needs and possibilities in the primary phase', in NEWTON, L.D. (ed.) *Primary Science: The Challenge of the 1990s*, Clevedon: Multilingual Matters, pp. 69–83.

SHERRINGTON, R. (ed.) (1993) *The ASE Primary Science Teachers' Handbook*, Hemel Hempstead: Simon and Schuster Education.

SKAMP, K.R. (1986) 'Investigating opportunities for learning science process skills', *Primary Science Review*, **2**, Autumn, pp. 10–11.

TEACHER TRAINING AGENCY (TTA) (1996) *Consultation Paper on Standards and A National Professional Qualification for Subject Leaders*, London: TTA.

WALSH, A. (1994) 'Today was another conceptual struggle', *Primary Science Review*, **33**, June, pp. 18–20.

WOLFENDALE, S. (1992) *Primary Schools and Special Needs*, London: Cassell.

Index

ORDER FORM

Post: *Customer Services Department, Falmer Press, Rankine Road, Basingstoke, Hampshire, RG24 8PR*
Tel: *(01256) 813000* **Fax**: *(01256) 479438*
E-mail: *book.orders@tandf.co.uk*

10% DISCOUNT AND FREE P&P FOR SCHOOLS OR INDIVIDUALS ORDERING THE COMPLETE SET
ORDER YOUR SET NOW. WITH CREDIT CARD PAYMENTS, YOU WON'T BE CHARGED TILL DESPATCH.

TITLE	DUE	ISBN	PRICE	QTY
SUBJECT LEADERS' HANDBOOKS SET		**(RRP £207.20)**	**£185.00**	
Coordinating Science	2/98	0 7507 0688 0	£12.95	
Coordinating Design and Technology	2/98	0 7507 0689 9	£12.95	
Coordinating Maths	2/98	0 7507 0687 2	£12.95	
Coordinating Physical Education	2/98	0 7507 0693 7	£12.95	
Coordinating History	2/98	0 7507 0691 0	£12.95	
Coordinating Music	2/98	0 7507 0694 5	£12.95	
Coordinating Geography	2/98	0 7507 0692 9	£12.95	
Coordinating English at Key Stage 1	4/98	0 7507 0685 6	£12.95	
Coordinating English at Key Stage 2	4/98	0 7507 0686 4	£12.95	
Coordinating IT	4/98	0 7507 0690 2	£12.95	
Coordinating Art	4/98	0 7507 0695 3	£12.95	
Coordinating Religious Education	Late 98	0 7507 0613 9	£12.95	
Management Skills for SEN Coordinators	Late 98	0 7507 0697 X	£12.95	
Building a Whole School Assessment Policy	Late 98	0 7507 0698 8	£12.95	
Curriculum Coordinator and OFSTED Inspection	Late 98	0 7507 0699 6	£12.95	
Coordinating Curriculum in Smaller Primary School	Late 98	0 7507 0700 3	£12.95	

I wish to pay by:

❑ Cheque *(Pay Falmer Press)*
❑ Pro-forma invoice
❑ Credit Card *(Mastercard / Visa / AmEx)*

Please add p&p
orders up to £25 — 10%
orders from £25 to £50 — 5%
orders over £50 — free

Value of Books	
P&P*	
Total	

Card Number _____ Expiry Date _____
Signature _____
Name _____ Title/Position _____
School _____
Address _____
_____
Postcode _____ Country _____
Tel no. _____ Fax _____
E-mail _____

☐ If you do not wish to receive further promotional information from the Taylor&Francis Group, please tick box.
All prices are correct at time of going to print but may change without notice

Ref: 1197BFSLAD